THE
CRUCIBLE'S
GREATEST
MATCHES

THE
CRUCIBLE'S
GREATEST
MATCHES

Forty Years of Snooker's World Championship in Sheffield

HECTOR NUNNS

First published by Pitch Publishing, 2017

Pitch Publishing
A2 Yeoman Gate
Yeoman Way
Worthing
Sussex
BN13 3QZ

www.pitchpublishing.co.uk
info@pitchpublishing.co.uk

ISBN 978-1-78531-284-7

Typesetting and origination by Pitch Publishing

Printed and bound in Great Britain by TJ International Ltd, Padstow

Contents

To Sarah, Rebecca and Rosie

Foreword

By World Snooker chairman Barry Hearn

W HEN Hector asked me if I would write the foreword for this book, I was only too happy to do so and agreed immediately.

Snooker's World Championship is one of the great sporting events of the year not just in the United Kingdom, but now followed worldwide by hundreds of millions of people.

And since 1977 it has taken place in a small arena in Sheffield, England going by the name of the Crucible Theatre, a true theatre of dreams for all professional snooker players.

There is little doubt that this iconic and uniquely atmospheric venue adds to the tournament itself, for the players, the television viewers, and also the thousands who make the annual pilgrimage to South Yorkshire to watch the action live.

There have been so many great matches at the Crucible over the years and I doubt you could find two people anywhere who would agree exactly on a long list of them. But you can have a go, and that is what Hector has done in this book, one that certainly includes several of the enduring classics that most aficionados like me would name.

It is a fine addition to the snooker literature out there, and a subject that was well worthy of the effort and overdue for more consideration. Each match is offered as a separate story and readers can cherry-pick and dip in and out of it at their leisure.

Everyone will have their own favourites, and there is something for everyone going right back to the early years, featuring the most famous names and contests the sport has seen in Sheffield. And as for those included or excluded that cause offence, that's a good pub argument waiting to happen!

Unlike a lot of sports snooker can be a slow burner, the tension builds minute by minute, frame by frame, hour by hour and especially at the Crucible where the matches are the longest we see. It is a great British eccentricity of an event, but a semi-final lasting three days? Tell that to the Americans!

But it is so English, who else would do it? A match at the Crucible is like reading a long book with a series of plot twists, and you are gripped but don't know until the final page what will happen.

My own greatest match at the Crucible is obviously a highly personal one, but it can only be and will always be the 1981 final between Steve Davis and Doug Mountjoy. It was a mission for us, the player and his manager, to win the World Championship.

When Steve won it, it was the culmination of everything he and I had dreamed about and worked towards. To this day it is the one sporting event I think about first, and stands out head and shoulders above the rest – and I have been involved in and attended a few of those.

And I can't lie, it was a pivotal moment in both our careers and I will never forget that or take it for granted. A couple of blokes who came from council houses, fulfilling a dream, the dream since Steve signed a contract with me up against a lamp post in Blackpool in 1978.

It wasn't panic but this was his chance in 1981, he had to do it now because he hadn't been the overnight sensation I thought he would be against the big boys.

I never sat in the arena for Steve's matches, but in that final session I did with my wife Susan, and as it got nearer the winning line I was telling myself not to do anything stupid. It might have also been a huge moment for me, but it was Steve's moment... And then of course he pots the pink and I am on the dance floor, hitting him with a rugby tackle that would have knocked out most second rows in what was the greatest sporting moment in my life.

In recent years one of the constants on the professional circuit has been the presence of Hector in the media centre or on the end of the phone, battling to get snooker coverage in the face of an ever more competitive marketplace, and with so many pages of national newspapers devoted to football.

His enthusiasm for the sport shines through. I know both he and the many playing legends interviewed for this book enjoyed the experience, and he is very well qualified to write this book having covered the sport, good stories and occasionally bad, for 15 years.

I hope you enjoy reading it,

Barry Hearn,

Chairman,

World Snooker,

January 2017.

Preamble
by Hector Nunns

I CAN still recall very clearly my own first visit to the Crucible Theatre to watch the World Championship live – even though the experience was thrillingly brief.

It was in 1996 and a good friend of mine Russ Bryan, who made the pilgrimage every year with his much-loved grandfather and knowing I was a huge fan and studying at that time at Sheffield University, suggested I meet up with them and come along.

My ticket was for the middle session of a best-of-25-frames quarter-final between two young pups with a bit of ability and these days a few trophies between them, a certain Ronnie O'Sullivan and John Higgins, both at that time without a world title but ready to challenge the 1990s hegemony of Stephen Hendry.

So the first frame I ever saw at the iconic venue was a characteristically effortless century break (102) from the man known to all as the Rocket, something that arguably set some kind of tone for much of what I was to see in later years both as a spectator and then for the past 15 years as a journalist covering the tournament.

Snooker is a sport that has captured my imagination ever since my late uncle James Nunns first let me loose on a full-size table at Effingham Golf Club in Surrey. I believe it is still there; the room was grand, and dark bar the actual table lighting, atmospheric and a little foreboding. I must have been about ten and although the game seemed impossible, the possibilities appeared limitless.

Preamble

I watched the World Championship on TV from 1979 but also saw snooker live at the old Wembley Conference Centre in the 1980s and early 1990s, sitting among sell-out 2,500 crowds for matches featuring the likes of Alex Higgins and Jimmy White. For those two in particular these tended to be raucous affairs that as a spectator often felt more like being in the away end at a football match.

But this, the Crucible, was different. Unlike at the Conference Centre, where you could barely see the balls if sitting right at the back, spectators from almost any vantage point felt as if they were part of the arena, so close were they to the action.

Those lucky individuals sitting on the front row could have reached out and touched the players, though that might have earned them a speedy exit from the premises.

A reverential hush descended as the play commenced, punctuated by shouts of support, bursts of applause and the obligatory 'oohs' and 'aahs' after pieces of fortune, good or bad, and bad misses. And all eyes were transfixed on the two young players and emerging talents on our side of the central dividing screen, the quarter-final being the last round with a two-table set-up.

And in this particular encounter there was plenty to applaud. Following O'Sullivan's opening contribution Scotland's Higgins, who had won the first session 5-3, hit straight back with a break of 94.

And in what seemed like the blink of an eye the frames raced by, three more 50+ breaks from O'Sullivan and further efforts of 104 and 70 from Higgins. The 'Wizard of Wishaw' won a high-quality second session by the same score, 5-3, to extend his overall lead to a commanding 10-6.

The players can't have actually been at the table for more than about an hour and a half in total, and the eight frames whistled by in what seemed the blink of an eye. Those around me exchanged knowing glances, recognising the level of what they had just seen. It was a far cry from some of the snooker produced by the master tacticians of a previous generation.

And you wandered out into the buzzing foyer thirsting for more and just wishing you had a ticket for the decisive and concluding final session. As it turned out that match turned into something of a classic itself, O'Sullivan roaring back to win seven of the last nine frames for a 13-12 victory.

The contest could easily have commanded a chapter to itself in this book, but has not on this occasion in what all will recognise is an exercise in total subjectivity.

We will move on later to exactly what might constitute a great snooker match – but why does the Crucible Theatre merit a book all to itself on the subject?

The famous theatre in Sheffield has since 1977 staged the World Championship, the biggest, best and final tournament of the season, and the one to which so many top players gear their whole campaign in order to be in peak form and condition as they attempt to lift that famous silver trophy.

Thanks to a deal signed in 2016 between World Snooker and Sheffield City Council, the event will now be staying certainly in the city until 2027 and at the Crucible for at least half of that time, warding off any interest at least for now to take the tournament to China or elsewhere in the snooker-playing world.

While this prompted the odd howl of outrage in sections of the Chinese media, the decision was greeted in most quarters with delight and relief by players, fans and administrators alike – from overseas as well as in the UK.

World Snooker chairman Barry Hearn is a businessman to the core, and showed in the years after he took the helm that he is not afraid of change, including venues and long-established formats of tournaments, if he feels that such alterations will generate interest, money, television audiences and ticket sales.

But the World Championship, Sheffield, the Crucible Theatre and the longest matches that make up snooker's supreme challenge were pointedly left alone – a special venue and tournament, deserving of being a special case.

Mark Williams of Wales is a phlegmatic character and the Welshman was, of course, the man that found himself in hot water after referring to the Crucible as a "s***hole" on social media on the eve of the 2012 World Championship and ended up having to apologise to staff at the theatre. The furore the incident stirred up showed, as much as anything, the peculiar hold the hallowed place has on the UK and wider world's psyche for 17 days in April and May.

Williams, whose head was never turned by his two world titles, has always been blessed with a deadpan sense of humour as well as a colourful turn of phrase and remains to this day baffled that such a throwaway remark could have caused such a media storm but news is often a product of its timing. The day before the World Championship starts, these things can get very big, very quickly.

The World Championship and the Crucible have no monopoly on great matches, and most reading this book will effortlessly recall plenty of classic encounters at other prestigious tournaments.

The invitational Masters has thrown up many examples, such as the John Higgins v Ronnie O'Sullivan final that provided a fitting curtain call for the old Wembley Conference Centre. Higgins trailed 60-0 in the decider but a trademark clutch break of 64 almost literally brought the house down. Steve Davis's comeback to win the 1997 Masters final at the age of 39 against O'Sullivan also springs to mind. So, too, the long-established UK Championship.

But if such encounters take place on the World Championship stage and at the Crucible, they are by their very nature often greater than would be the case elsewhere.

It is the ultimate proving ground, with the greatest spotlight and scrutiny and pressure on the players, and because of the status and stature of the tournament and the worldwide profile of the event, a classic match there will invariably burrow deeper into the general consciousness.

A longer format is part of that, of course, as it allows the narrative of a match to ebb and flow. A shock win in a best-of-seven-frame clash in a minor ranking event elsewhere holds nowhere near the value of one claimed over the best-of-25 frames at the Crucible.

If an extended number of frames is one of the contributors to making a match great, then what are the others?

If you reflect on what matches you regard as great not only in snooker but in other sports, there are a plethora of factors that can make it so – and not all of them relate directly to the action on the table. There are considerations of context, personalities, rivalry, history and even nostalgia.

At the most basic level, it can be the pure undiluted and uninhibited quality of play on show, and ideally though not necessarily from both players at the same time.

Several of the matches between, for example, record seven-time world champion Stephen Hendry and O'Sullivan would slot neatly into this category, notably semi-finals played at the Crucible. More recently the World Championship semi-final between Judd Trump and China's Ding Junhui in 2011 was a joy to behold, and a modern-day classic.

Often in sport the media are too reliant on statistics, used as a 'filler' rather than hard news reporting or an evocative description of what is occurring. Just think of the hours of coverage the organisation OPTA provide for Sky Sports News on football.

But there are sports, and snooker, baseball and cricket spring to mind, where the statistics regularly are the story and this is especially true in matches of rare quality.

You can see the centuries, the 50+ breaks, the maximum 147s, they are there in black and white on the tournament director's match sheet at the end.

If all visits to the table result in a frame-winning break and one-visit snooker, entertainment and an appreciation of the potting and positional play arts is guaranteed. The trading of big breaks in the arena is the closest snooker gets to a couple of boxing heavyweights slugging it out in the ring.

There is, of course though, more to it than that when it comes to great matches and the most intense drama in snooker is often borne out of errors and mistakes.

If there is one myth that has grown up around the fabled 1985 final between Steve Davis and Dennis Taylor, it is that the match was of high quality. It was not, with no century breaks. And yet it is rightly the most remembered and talked-about single encounter in snooker history, and an iconic sporting moment.

The drama stemmed from many sources, and clearly the nature of the finish was paramount. After two days, four sessions and 35 frames, to have the World Championship decided on the final black after the world No.1 and dominant player of his generation had missed a chance to clinch the title took the thrill level off the scale.

And the match was great for any number of other reasons. The popular underdog won against all the odds, a classic sporting story template. Taylor came back from a seemingly hopeless position in the final, trailing 8-0 at one stage, for the most unlikely of world titles. Davis, going for a fourth world title and a third in a row, for once showed some flaws and chinks in the armour in the heat of battle. And the celebrations were unbridled and clearly unrehearsed.

A nation was gripped. The TV audience of 18.5million that stayed up until well after midnight to watch the thrilling denouement has often since been unfairly used as a stick with which to beat snooker – but quite why such a high water-mark should be seen in this light is bizarre. The nature of television has changed beyond all recognition since those four-channel days in the UK, with hundreds to choose from.

Snooker is thriving in many parts of the world helped by the efforts of Eurosport and CCTV, but it can struggle to make headway with some sections of the media in its former UK heartland away from the World Championship, and even during it. Whatever lies at the heart of this, and snobbery is sometimes advanced as a reason when the sport still produces TV audiences in the millions others would die for, it is through no fault of the current crop of players' on-table efforts. The spectacle they are providing is of a consistently high standard.

Sometimes a match can look great on paper in advance, thanks to big-name participants and a previous head-to-head record that suggests a classic can reasonably be expected. How often do you see a football fixture between rivals hyped to the nth degree on 'Super

Sunday', only for the actual offering to disappoint. But when such clashes do deliver, they are special. And there are many, many more factors that perhaps not in isolation but when taken in conjunction with others can add to the mix. A clash of playing styles never goes amiss, summoning up matches between the likes of Alex Higgins and Cliff Thorburn, Steve Davis and Jimmy White, and more recently O'Sullivan and Mark Selby.

A new name for the wider public to conjure with can add something special, thinking here of Trump in the 2011 final against Higgins, and also Martin Gould's match with Neil Robertson in 2010. The Australian, with at the time of writing still the single world title to his name, must shudder when he thinks about how close he was to going out that year.

When players have previous history, and the latest instalment is one of a series going back years, the result can be explosive. In the same way that anticipation soared ahead of Roger Federer and Rafa Nadal's tennis matches, or the fights between Marvin Hagler, Sugar Ray Leonard, Thomas Hearns and Roberto Duran, summit meetings of snooker greats often produce classic moments.

On a similar theme, the 2007 quarter-final between Matthew Stevens and Shaun Murphy was not only a superb match in its own right, its significance was only enhanced by the fact that the Magician had won a final between the two of them only two years earlier. Context matters.

In any sport a shock creates waves and headlines and snooker is no different. The first-round 10-1 win for Tony Knowles over defending champion Steve Davis in 1982 was not only an early example of the 'Crucible Curse' affecting first-time winners of the World Championship, but a genuinely jaw-dropping result. Ding Junhui's first-round defeat at the hands of Michael Wasley in 2014 was another in the same bracket.

Does a match have to be close to be great? I would say not, although many might disagree and we all appreciate the nerve-shredding tension of a deciding frame after a long struggle building to a thrilling climax.

Preamble

To use a horseracing analogy, I have been to the Cheltenham Festival and other meetings to see magnificent horses at their best, wanting to see it leave the rest ten lengths adrift and show just how good they really were.

For Kauto Star and Best Mate in the Gold Cup, or Sprinter Sacre and Moscow Flyer in the Champion Chase, read O'Sullivan against Hendry in the 2004 Crucible semi-final. This was a thoroughbred at the peak of his powers, humbling a previously invincible champion 17-4.

I would argue this was an example of a match that was great in a one-sided sense, a masterclass demonstration – as were in their own way Steve Davis's 18-3 final win over John Parrott, and Hendry's 18-5 victory over Jimmy White.

The stage of the tournament at which a match occurs is also clearly important, and there can be seen in this selection a clear bias towards encounters in the final or latter stages at the Crucible. It was noted earlier that the pressure and spotlight as well as the potential rewards, glory and kudos are greater at the World Championship, and much the same can be said the further a player advances through the draw towards the final.

And magical moments can only enhance a match that is already of high quality. Cliff Thorburn's epic match with Terry Griffiths in 1983 would have been memorable enough for finishing at 3.51am in front of a handful of stalwarts. The fact that (much) earlier in the clash the Canadian had made the first 147 maximum break seen at the Crucible demands its inclusion.

It feels slightly wrong that the likes of Williams, Mark Selby and Stuart Bingham do not feature given some of their extraordinary recent exploits at the Crucible – others might have included some of their matches. I would certainly subscribe to the view advanced by Hearn in the foreword that this is more the start of a decent pub argument than any kind of definitive work.

And there are so many other fantastic Crucible matches that I either watched myself at the time, or have been made aware of since, so let's list a few of them that were close.

Terry Griffiths v Alex Higgins quarter-final in 1979; Cliff Thorburn v Tony Knowles semi-final in 1983; Jimmy White v Kirk Stevens semi-final in 1984; Tony Knowles v Jimmy White quarter-final in 1985; John Parrott v Steve James, first round in 1989; Matthew Stevens v Peter Ebdon semi-final in 2002; Ronnie O'Sullivan v Stephen Hendry semi-final 2002; Ian McCulloch v Mark Williams, last 16 in 2005; Nigel Bond v Stephen Hendry, first round 2006; Ali Carter v Joe Perry semi-final in 2008; John Higgins v Jamie Cope, last 16 2011; Ronnie O'Sullivan v Joe Perry last 16, 2014 and the final that year between O'Sullivan and Mark Selby.

Gaining an insight into the minds of top sportspeople before, during and after they compete under the most intense pressure has always fascinated me and hopefully the series of interviews undertaken for this book will offer some kind of window into how the very best snooker players cope with the mental challenges, and deal with victory and agonising defeat.

Covering snooker has been an immense privilege for me, ever since my esteemed predecessor as correspondent at the *Daily Express*, John 'Tex' Hennessey, threw a World Championship accreditation form at me over the sub-editing desk as he was leaving the newspaper and said, "There you go, you might be needing that." The long snooker-related chats on a late shift were not wasted.

As a job it has been like any other; many moments of great pleasure, joy and satisfaction, along with the occasional frustration. I have made many friends along the way, both in the worlds of snooker and sports journalism, and got to travel to some incredible places – notably China, a country that is now so important for the sport, and India.

Being from a school of journalism that believes it is all about the main actors in sport, ie the players, and that the media is there to report on them rather than be personalities in their own right, I have always been hugely appreciative of the players' efforts to make themselves available and try and represent their sport and help it compete with all the others vying for space in newspapers.

Preamble

Almost without exception, even the game's legends will answer phones and go beyond their contractual obligations for the benefit of snooker, the game they love, and it is to their immense credit because clearly along the way there will be the odd story that ruffles feathers.

And for that generally over the last 15 years, and specifically for the time willingly given to assist in the interviews that form the basis of this book, I am extremely grateful.

If there is one thing that has astounded me writing this book, it is the clarity of memory of shots and matches from 20, 25, 30 or more years ago from the players who took part. Often I would call with no notice expecting to request they have a think about it and I would get back to them – but usually there was no need.

The notion that snooker is one of the most mentally demanding of sports is not a new one – I and other observers have been claiming that for years. But the extent to which in the great Crucible matches good and bad shots, and key moments, observations and feelings from decades previously stay burnished into the brain was more of a surprise.

That warm thanks extends to those in the non-playing snooker family who have assisted in the realisation of the book (even unknowingly), including Barry Hearn for kindly agreeing to write the foreword, Ivan Hirschowitz, Brandon Parker, Mike Watterson, Pat Wells, Phil Yates, Chris Downer, Ron Florax and Tai Chengzhe – as well as picture providers Ernie Whitehead, Trevor Smith, PA Images and Getty Images.

The fan's view pieces provided by my good friend John Airey, who has forgotten more about snooker than I will ever know, for two of the most famous Crucible finals – the 1985 black-ball epic between Taylor and Davis, and the 1994 showpiece between Hendry and Jimmy White – are superb. I would like to express my gratitude to him for penning them. They must be worth a beer or two in the Mercure Hotel bar. Another falling into the 'experts' expert' category is Matt Huart, huge thanks to him for his proofreading of the manuscript, and other helpful suggestions.

There are more people to thank. Paul and Jane Camillin at Pitch Publishing gave me some freedom but also nursed me through my first book with skill and understanding, and Duncan Olner came up with the cover design concepts that also frightened the life out of me, bringing home the fact I now had to get this written. Thanks also to Graham Hales and Dean Rockett.

But most of all I would like to thank my wife Sarah and daughters Rebecca and Rosie for their unfailing love, support and enthusiasm throughout the process, despite taking myself off to the cabin 'office' in the garden for long spells over Christmas and the New Year.

As a nostalgia victim myself, I hope the matches featured stir up a few good memories and that there is at least something for everyone within – and apologise in advance for any outrage provoked by glaring omissions.

Please enjoy reading the book,

Hector Nunns

Chapter 1

The World Championship finds a spiritual home

"My wife Carole had been to the theatre – she knew what I had in mind for a World Championship and came back one day saying she had seen the perfect venue for snooker"

WHEN looking at the history of snooker's World Championship, you might easily conclude that 1976 – when the tournament was staged at the Wythenshawe Forum in Manchester – could best be described as 1 BC, where BC stands for 'Before Crucible'.

From 1977 the greatest and final event on the season's calendar has taken place at a small theatre in the South Yorkshire city of Sheffield in the United Kingdom, a place where history has been made, legends created, dreams made real and plenty more hopes dashed.

The word 'Crucible', at least to fans of sport outside a theatre-going community equally in love with the place at the bottom of Tudor Square, has become almost synonymous with the game itself – as much as Wimbledon for tennis, Augusta for the Masters golf, and Silverstone for the British Grand Prix in Formula One.

For those 17 days in April and May a tournament over distance which can even be seen in certain quarters as quaint, eccentric and anachronistic in today's world of reduced concentration spans provides the supreme test for a snooker player over matches that can take up to three days, and captures the imagination of the world.

For this period a very different kind of stage to the usual one affords its star performers the opportunity to delight the audience, or drive it to distraction. There are plots, pots and pathos in abundance, and regulars at the venue come to know every nook and cranny, from the location of the various players' guest boxes, to the seats that view over both sides of the partition, to the best places to lurk with an autograph book.

One of my own favourite Crucible traditions was the poster on the side of the church opposite the stage door at World Championship time that read: 'Without God, you're snookered', now sadly taken out of commission.

And yet it is only by the moment of inspiration of Carole Watterson and the vision, risk-taking and perseverance of husband Mike, together with the subsequent efforts of so many more, that the Crucible ever became the spiritual home of snooker and the setting for not just the great matches featured in this book, but so much more besides.

The 1976 World Championship, despite being the first to be sponsored by tobacco giant Embassy and producing a good level of snooker, had not been considered a huge success as an event. Split over two locations, the Middlesbrough Town Hall and the Wythenshawe Forum, which hosted the final itself, the showpiece was won 27-16 by Ray Reardon against Alex Higgins.

With real doubts and concerns over the 1977 tournament Watterson, a businessman with diverse interests from cars to recycling, a fine amateur player and already a promoter of snooker exhibition matches, started to take an interest.

He takes up the story. "Wythenshawe was appalling for snooker really, it was like an aircraft hangar," said Watterson.

"My wife Carole had been to see a play at the Crucible Theatre a short while before we were talking about it, and she knew from my discussions the kind of venue I had in mind if the opportunity came along to put on a World Championship. She came home one day and said she had seen the perfect venue for snooker.

"So on my way to the Gimcrack meeting at York I dropped in at the Crucible and spent ten minutes with Arnold Elliman, the theatre manager. I knew we needed 36 feet to get two tables in and the necessary room either side, and a thin partition but at first he said 'I think it's 34 feet, but I'll check that.'

"And luckily when he asked Malcolm, the stage manager, it turned out it was exactly 36 feet and just what we needed. The stage had apparently been designed to that length because that was the time it took an actor walking slowly across it making a speech from a Shakespeare play from start to finish. So that was fortuitous, and it worked out perfectly. My first thought when I first walked into the place though, it just knocked me out and I remember thinking so clearly, 'This is the kind of place I would love to play in as a player, and watch as a spectator,' and I knew I wanted to get hold of the deal to stage the World Championship.

"We didn't have the current practice room facility then because that was a separate theatre called the Studio Theatre. But being a theatre the dressing rooms were just off stage, and that worked.

"We were a bit restricted for space as today, and to start with we were interlopers as we were not producing anything theatrical. But as the snooker event grew, and brought good publicity for the theatre and the city, then that changed."

So how did a Chesterfield owner of businesses selling and repairing cars, and selling computer materials to wastepaper companies to be recycled as envelopes, come to win the rights to stage snooker's greatest tournament at the Crucible?

"John Pulman, a close friend who was involved with the WPBSA, had been staying with Carole and I in 1976," Watterson said. "He told me, 'We are in big trouble for next year, we have no promoter, no venue, no sponsor, no TV, nothing,' and this was in the August.

"I am not saying there would have been no Championship, but it would have been cobbled together at the last minute at somewhere like the Selly Oak British Legion where it had been four years before, with some seating two bricks and a plank.

"I stuck a bid in with none of these things in place, underwriting it with my own money. I guaranteed £17,000 in prize money, and other costs including venue hire another £13,000 or so, making the total I could have lost £30,000. In today's money that would be around £500,000.

"My bank and solicitor confirmed I was good for the money, I think I paid a £2,000 deposit, and it was ratified in the November. From November to March when the qualifiers started wasn't long, and Embassy didn't come back on board until the February.

"Rex Williams had asked me to give Embassy first refusal before it was offered to another sponsor, so I did that and waited until the absolute death and had to give Peter Dyke, their then sponsorship manager, a strict deadline.

"And it wasn't always easy dealing with Rex Williams. He had a beef with me because I got given the great Joe Davis's famous CUE1 car registration plate, something Joe had kindly promised me.

"When I went in to show Peter Dyke the theatre it was a no-smoking venue in the theatre and auditorium itself, and I remember standing in front of a 'No Smoking' sign while we were talking, and I don't think he was that happy afterwards but luckily it got signed.

"Funnily enough people will remember players such as Alex Higgins smoking in the auditorium at the Crucible, but they were allowed to. It came under the same kind of loophole that allowed actors to smoke as they were 'stage props'. And the police had to accept that.

"Ray Reardon rang me up and asked, 'What the bloody hell are you doing…and where's Sheffield?' And that was occasionally what you got at the start."

Reardon, of course, was to become rather better acquainted with the Steel City when winning the sixth and last of his world titles the following year in 1978 with a 25-18 victory over Perrie Mans, not to mention helping mentor Ronnie O'Sullivan to a second title in 2004.

With the deal done with the WPBSA and a venue sorted, there were still the small matters of sponsorship and BBC TV coverage to be arranged, if the £30,000 guarantee put up by Watterson was not to disappear into a financial black hole.

Nick Hunter, a senior BBC sports producer in Manchester, was key to the TV negotiations.

Watterson said: "The BBC had covered the final in 1976, and Nick Hunter, who was a senior producer, initially said the Crucible was 'too good' for snooker when I got in touch and showed him the venue, and said 'Have you thought of a Gerry Cottle's Circus tent?'

"I started laughing, but that reflected the view of some of the venues that had been used. And he agreed to coverage for the last three days. The final session of the final would be live, and the semi-final highlights would be shown over the rest of the three days of the final.

"And the format to get strategic finish times for TV was set up that year, tweaked in 1978 – and that latter one is pretty much the format in use today."

And the lighting, probably taken for granted by many of today's professionals, raised difficulties for those more accustomed to setting it up for the *Pot Black* one-frame programme at Pebble Mill.

"We had a lighting meeting in March of 1977 together with Mike Green of the WPBSA, Nick Hunter of the BBC, and a *Pot Black* lighting engineer, and another lighting engineer John Crowther and I took my cue as requested so we could do a few tests," Watterson recalled.

"But the lighting for *Pot Black* was simply not suitable for the World Championship. It was no good, the whole place was lit up like Blackpool Illuminations. The number of lights shining on the balls from all around, the balls looked like flying saucers. So by turning everything off bar the lights over the table, it was far better.

"And there were other changes for the following year, using neon lighting and diffusers and lowering the canopy overhead to get the best effect."

The larger the World Championship has become and the more countries take TV pictures or send media to the event, and the more people want to host corporate hospitality functions at a major event on the sporting calendar, and the more fans want to buy tickets, so the limitations of the building itself and arena capacity can get highlighted.

When Mark Williams, another multiple winner of the title, made his unfortunate comment about the venue on the eve of the 2012 tournament, he was genuinely stunned at the furious reaction, much of it from people who were not familiar with his sense of humour, laconic delivery and occasional industrial language. Plenty were very defensive about their favourite sporting arena.

But somewhere in that 'Williams-speak' and beyond the offence caused and taken by the theatre's management and governing bodies there was a half-legitimate observation about the facilities compared not only to other venues used by snooker, but other sporting events.

That first year saw Watterson find his own office, and a press room – also upstairs – albeit one that was tiny by today's standards.

"The first press room was upstairs and there wasn't much there – a couple of telephones, and you had usually Ted Corbett, Janice Hale and Clive Everton," he said. "That was the press, nothing like today, and it wasn't until the second year we had monitors installed so we could see what was happening in the auditorium. I used the room that was called Room 10, which had racks where the bands for the theatre shows used to hang their instruments."

But the real proof of the Crucible pudding in 1977 was always going to be in the tournament itself, the spectacle it provided, the memories made, the personalities on show, the tickets sold, satisfaction among sponsors and broadcasters and the quality of the matches.

And for Watterson the 'Field of Dreams' moment and relief when on that first morning, Monday 18 April at around 10.40am, the audience came has remained with him to this day.

The World Championship finds a spiritual home

"The first two matches on the first day in 1977 were Fred Davis against John Pulman, and Ray Reardon against Patsy Fagan," he said. "I stood on the stage about 10.40am when they opened the doors and had my fingers crossed, praying, 'God I hope someone turns up.'

"And when they opened up about 200 people came in and I remember thinking, 'I love every one of you.' There had been about £1,000 worth of ticket sales, but mainly towards the end of the tournament and a lot of people were paying on the door. I think it was 75 pence for early-round matches.

"And there was a cracking match between Alex Higgins and Doug Mountjoy in that first week, a very close match, and maybe the first time the place was full and buzzing. Doug won the match 13-12, and potted an amazing blue down the side cushion that helped him win. Perrie Mans said at the time, 'That's not fair, you can't pot balls like that!' because the tables in South Africa did not allow that.

"And of course we got a good final, with John Spencer beating Cliff Thorburn 25-21 over the three days.

"There were only 16 players that first year, but the exposure convinced others to turn professional, and the number was growing as they all wanted to play at the Crucible, and by 1982 that had gone up to 32, the same as it is today.

"I think I made about a £12,000 profit that first year – but then lost £5,000 on the UK Championship that I promoted later that year. It summed up perfectly the swings and roundabouts of promoting events.

"The greatest indicator of success to me was the enthusiasm of the crowds at the Crucible, and the appreciation of the players. And we knew once the BBC started to cover the whole event, a format could be worked out to engineer good finishes at the right times for TV."

Needless to say when Watterson in recent years has made the short trip to Sheffield and the Crucible from his Chesterfield home just over the county border in Derbyshire, it is with a sense of pride that he surveys the tournament in its long-time home.

"Of course when I look at the event still being staged there and some of the things players and fans say about it, it does give you a sense of satisfaction and achievement to have played some part in creating that," he said. "Of course you feel some pride.

"And the profile and success of the Crucible helped the snooker boom in the 1980s, with TV viewing figures up to around 13 million by 1981.

"I would say that by about 1979 the Crucible started to be taken more seriously and seen as a real part of the sporting landscape in this country, that marked the start of the bonanza and you could see it in the World Championship attendances and viewing figures."

Surely with all that history and tradition the event could never move away? The announcement by World Snooker chairman Barry Hearn in 2016 that the tournament would remain at the Crucible for at least another five years and in Sheffield for at least another ten was greeted with both delight and sighs of relief, even in some of those countries who might be interested in staging a World Championship elsewhere.

The commercial nature of sport makes it almost impossible to ever say 'never' about anything and the Crucible's capacity of just 980 that contributes to the intimacy in the arena hands promoters a headache, only in the sense that you might easily sell 5,000 tickets for a final or other big match.

Ronnie O'Sullivan, a multiple world champion who features heavily in these pages, has always loved actually playing at the Crucible even if sustaining form and concentration for the duration of the event has occasionally been more of a struggle – and has made the arena as special as most through his efforts. On the Crucible's commercial conundrum, he observed: "I think there may inevitably be a move away from the Crucible at some point.

"There will come a point where they want 128 players at one venue like Wimbledon, and that won't be this one. It is a great playing venue but not the best venue for getting in and out of, and for the capacity.

The World Championship finds a spiritual home

"As the game grows and prize money grows I'm sure they might want to expand to somewhere where they can sell 4,000 or 5,000 tickets for a match – which we could."

However, the 1997 world champion Ken Doherty of Ireland, now a successful BBC presenter and commentator, was certain the case to keep the blue-riband tournament where it is was unanswerable.

Doherty said: "Some things money can't buy – they are just more important than that, and the Crucible is one.

"You could play in a place where you had 5,000 people and make more money – but would it generate the same atmosphere? Sometimes places can be too big. Even at the old Wembley Conference Centre where we used to play the Masters, it was brilliant when it was full, but some early-round matches fell a bit flat.

"Only if Jimmy White or Ronnie O'Sullivan or Steve Davis was playing was the atmosphere great. At the Crucible, it is great for every match.

"I am very nostalgic about the World Championship, about the Crucible, and the city. Okay, behind the scenes the scope for large-scale hospitality is more difficult.

"But you can't move the Masters golf from Augusta. I am all for it staying here as long as possible, though I know there will be temptations to move it elsewhere in the UK or the world.

"I just prefer it here. There is a commercial pressure and that side of it will make commercial decisions. But I hope they consider all aspects, and for me it wouldn't have the feel of the World Championship anywhere else.

"For fans and players it is like a pilgrimage, from all over the world. I'm just an old nostalgic fool that loves it. And as a player, there are just so many memories here. Every time you walk through those curtains, they come flooding in to your mind.

"You really feel them around the place, walking down the corridors, around the city – and your personal ones. And I have great memories of the theatre."

Everyone has their own great memories of the Crucible, and hopefully the matches featured in this book will stir a few.

Chapter 2

Cliff Thorburn v Alex Higgins, 1980, the final

*"I looked in the mirror, slapped myself
around a bit and screamed at my reflection
until my face went purple, shouting 'What
are you doing, this is your time'"*

THE first encounter featured in this book examines a marked clash of playing styles, some real personal animosity, the People's Champion, the first overseas world champion, a televised storming of the Iranian Embassy in London by the SAS… and all that is before actually considering how a ball was potted or a frame won.

The already legendary Alex Higgins of Northern Ireland was into his third World Championship final, going for a second world title after beating John Spencer at the Selly Park British Legion in 1972.

The 'Hurricane', a perfectly apt and well-deserved nickname first given to Higgins according to legend by John Taylor writing in the Blackburn local newspaper, was at the same time the most talented, adored (but not always adorable), charismatic, unorthodox, controversial and irreverent showman ever to have figured among the ranks of snooker professionals up until that moment – and quite possibly for all time.

Growing up on the streets of Belfast and having honed his skills in the billiard halls on the Falls and Shankhill Roads and elsewhere in the city, Higgins got an early compulsion to become a jockey out of his system by the age of 15, and returning to his other 'first love' made such a good job of it after moving to the north-west of England that he became the youngest ever snooker world champion at that time with the 37-32 win over Spencer.

Comparisons with Manchester United and Northern Ireland footballer George Best were almost inevitable, and not long in coming. As well as the home city, there was the genius, the flair, the unpredictable nature, the gambling, the drinking, the womanising and the difficulties with authority.

Higgins was no respecter of how the game had been played until that point, drawing in a whole new generation of fans with his ground-breaking and compelling approach, nor the way the sport was administered.

And Higgins, like Jimmy White and Ronnie O'Sullivan after him so fast around the table and drawn like a moth to a flame to the attacking option available, both lived and loved to entertain the public almost more than the actual winning itself – something that was to endear him to millions but also hurt his CV, not least in this very match.

Up against him was Canadian Cliff Thorburn, who came to be known to all as the Grinder, and perfectly happy to trade safety shots in a prolonged tactical battle before pouncing to pick up any pieces left by a demoralised opponent.

Thorburn was 32, from Victoria in British Columbia and had a pool-hall background and temperament that would serve him well in snooker. After turning professional in 1972 too late to play in the World Championship that year, Thorburn had reached the final in 1977, losing out to close friend John Spencer.

Higgins had enjoyed a fine season in 1979–80, winning three titles – most recently the British Gold Cup at the Assembly Rooms in Derby, where he beat Ray Reardon 5-1 – and reaching the final in three other tournaments. Thorburn had won two events, his home Canadian Open tournament with a win over Terry Griffiths, and the Canadian Professional Championship, defeating compatriot Jim Wych 9-6.

Now 31, Higgins had already marked down the up-and-coming Steve Davis and his manager Barry Hearn as threats to his playing success, and off-table earning power. And when the World Championship came around in April, a grudge quarter-final clash always seemed a possibility. Higgins edged past Tony Meo 10-9 in round one, before beating Perrie Mans 13-6 to set up a tie against the Nugget.

As Higgins relates in his book *My Story – From The Eye Of The Hurricane* written with Sean Boru, "I gave Steve what for…I was happy to wipe the smile off the face of Barry Hearn." Following a 13-9 victory he turned to Davis and said, as it turned out prophetically, "Never mind Steve, maybe next year." Davis did indeed win in 1981 – the first of six world titles.

Next up for Higgins was Kirk Stevens, a fellow free spirit, and a 16-13 victory saw him through to the final. It had been four years since Higgins had last been in a world final in 1976, losing to Reardon, but he was now married to Lynn, and she was expecting a baby.

Again from *My Story*, Higgins relates: "I felt good, the time felt right and as we went to bed the night before the final Lynn cuddled me and said she was so happy for me. I was happy for us both and for our little baby growing inside her. 'I'm doing this for you, babe,' I said through tears of joy and she squeezed me tighter. I felt safe in her arms, confident I would win the title."

When Thorburn reached the final in 1977, that achievement represented by his own admission almost the sum of his ambition, having set that as a career goal after playing in his first World Championship in 1973.

This time, after wins over Doug Mountjoy (13-10), Jim Wych (13-6), and David Taylor (16-7), things were different. Thorburn believed he had what it took to beat Higgins, who started the match a clear favourite.

And unlike so many who cut Higgins plenty of slack for his errant behaviour, perhaps in the belief that his brashness and play was making the snooker cake that much bigger for them all to share, Thorburn gave him short shrift, the result of an acute personality clash.

So mellow with the majority of his tour rivals, Higgins was the one that made Thorburn see red, something that was to occasionally lead to violent altercations during their careers. And this final was conducted with barely a word exchanged between the pair.

"I probably made a naïve mistake when I turned professional back in 1972, it is important when you get goals to have someone there giving you sensible advice," said Thorburn.

"My goal to myself was to get to the World Championship final within my first five tournaments. I didn't even really think about winning it.

"John Spencer had been a very important figure in getting me to turn pro in 1972, but it was too late to play in the World Championship that year. And I had gone on to play John in the final in 1977 at the Crucible.

"Now I had got there again in 1980. I remember talking to the journalist Ted Corbett and he asked me how I felt – and this time I told him that I felt I would win this thing.

"Alex and I had had a couple of incidents along the way, every time I played him there was always something that wasn't right and I was the type of guy that didn't take any crap from him.

"We settled down on tour not really talking, but nodding, and shaking hands before and after a match. I hadn't really been that way with anyone else in my life, but he was quite the character as they say.

"And I have never seen anyone try as hard as him to win a match. It wasn't everything, it was the only thing.

"I have always believed that the fact we weren't talking helped me quite a lot in that final. I had trouble playing good friends of mine, and found it harder to focus. Playing someone I actually disliked was easier. The best we got along was the six years we didn't speak!

"I think Alex often wanted to see how far he could push me, and you just don't take that. If I had been British I might have let him get away with more.

"And I have always thought the game compromised with him early in his career, thinking that he was good for the sport. If they had got tougher earlier with him, banned him for six months, he might have been a better person.

"We just didn't get along and he said some terrible things, but he had a chip on his shoulder and it was difficult."

If Thorburn had a problem with Higgins, for many fans and players alike the Hurricane was the man that was taking snooker to a new dimension with a breathtaking array of shot-making, and a swagger that cried out 'I am a superstar'.

That saw him attract an almost fanatical support, and not only among Irish followers from north and south of the border, but a genuine following for this man who appeared to be challenging the established order in just about every way imaginable, and shared vices and foibles that the ordinary man – and in those days it was largely men – could relate to.

Thorburn was popular even in the UK, but not to that extent and the Crucible crowd was very much behind Higgins, willing him on to a second world title. And things started well for the mercurial maverick of the green baize. Higgins moved into a 4-1 lead, and breaks of 93 and 81 helped him stand 6-3 ahead after the first session.

As Thorburn suggested years later, Higgins' sheer will to win this match saw him temper some of his more natural attacking instincts and play a brand of pragmatic snooker, mixing attack with defence and tactical acumen, an approach that saw him move to first 7-3 up and then 9-5 with four frames left on the first day.

A continuation of that policy may well have seen Higgins move even further ahead, but the performer and crowd-pleaser in him took over at a crucial stage of the match, and wild attempted pots opened the door for Thorburn, a chance he was only too happy to take. If Higgins had taken liberties with his opponent, it had come back to bite him.

In *My Story* Higgins says: "I had abandoned the strategically sound attack-and-defence approach and started to simply attack, attack, attack almost as if I was in an exhibition, playing long shots to impress the crowd. Normally I was the better tactician, knowing when to play safe and when to go for the jugular – but not in this match."

And as he told BBC presenter David Vine afterwards, "I have had disappointments before but I will bounce back. I lost the match from 7-3 and 9-5 in front, and my old crowd-pleasing thing came back again. It's hard to live with but I do, and I'll bounce back."

Thorburn also recalls that phase of the contest as being crucial, but played in an atmosphere that bore no relation to his only previous appearance in the final. "The match started and I was down early on, 9-5 during the second session on day one before I got it back to 9-9 overnight," he said.

"And it was so different from the 1977 final, playing a good friend in John Spencer where we were laughing and joking despite competing hard.

"I was pulling back, that was my nature at the time, and I am still like that now when I play golf. So I was in good shape, and even when he pulled away I always thought I could catch him. I had a game where I could shut him out, I was just a bad starter so often in matches.

"And that means sometimes you have more left in the tank at the end. It was blood and guts stuff out there and that suited me, also being the Canadian against the People's Champion – he'd go to the washroom and get cheered back in by everyone."

Higgins was later to admit that, strongly believing he would still win even starting the second day of the final level at 9-9, he may not have sufficiently respected the Canadian, something that invariably leads to a payback in one form or another in any sport.

From 11-11 there was never more than a frame in it until 16-16, Higgins taking advantage of a missed brown from Thorburn to level things up once again with just two frames required by either for the title. And it was a moment that was to prove pivotal, as a wound-up Thorburn departed the arena to try and simultaneously calm himself down after losing a frame he felt he should have won to stand at 17-15, and gee himself up for the finale.

"I missed a brown to lose the frame and be pulled back to 16-16 and I went to the washroom," Thorburn said. "I had to get out of there after missing a chance to go 17-15. As I had walked out four guys in Alex T-shirts were saying so I could hear, 'You've got him now, Alex.'

"I looked in the mirror, slapped myself around a bit and screamed at my reflection until my face went purple, shouting 'What are you doing, this is your time – go out there and do what you are capable of doing!' I'd recommend it, it was better than taking a deep breath.

"I think it got a lot of bad stuff out of my system, and I went back out there and made breaks of 119 and 51 to win 18-16. And for that 119, one of my best ever breaks and the highest of the match, the black was on the cushion until the end.

"The powers of concentration were good. I could have an hour-long frame and then go out and make a century, and others – including Alex – could do the same.

"In the last frame I made a couple of plants where they were a way apart, and he hardly had a shot. John Spencer was peeking around the curtain on the colours, he knew it was a big deal for me.

"I actually got down to pot the final black and then got up again thinking, 'What are you doing, who cares about the black, you have already won!' and went over to Alex, and there was a sort of a hug – after all, it had been a hell of a match.

"People often think it was Alex that called me the Grinder, but it was David Vine who came up with it in the interview after the final.

"So that was me on top of the world. I did read afterwards that Alex said he threw it away from 9-5, but if you look at the breaks after that I had plenty more over 45 than he did.

"I played very well and kept him out. I genuinely don't think he thought I had a chance against him in that final, even though I had beaten him in other tournaments.

"Holding the trophy and winning the World Championship gave me the most satisfaction. I knew I could beat Alex again, and the money was nice and I know I spent it, but the trophy was it for me, fulfilling the dream and I had good years after that."

Higgins of course had other fabulous moments at the Crucible, but this was to be Thorburn's day as he became the first player from outside the UK to win the World Championship – given a widespread reluctance to officially acknowledge the win for Australia's Horace Lindrum in a field of just two in 1952.

And BBC television coverage in that final session was also famously interrupted for live pictures of the storming of the Iranian Embassy by the SAS, following a six-day siege. Operation Nimrod began at around 7.30pm on 5 May, and even that threw up an unlikely snooker-related anecdote.

Thorburn said: "We had been aware of the siege, it had been going on for five days from the start of the semi-finals, and there was extra security at the Crucible that day. They cleaned lobby areas out and there seemed to be security guys walking around kicking a few bags – things have probably come a long way since then!

"One thing I was told was that one of the SAS guys who got hurt didn't want to go to hospital, but back to the barracks to watch the end of our final. And the story went that Margaret Thatcher came round to congratulate the soldiers on the end of the siege and sat and watched the final with this one for a while. I don't know how true that is, but who would make that up?"

But the sweetest moment for Thorburn on the night? Well, that might just have been making a mess of the celebratory cake that Higgins, slightly prematurely, had ordered to be brought to his dressing room with the match still on a knife-edge at 16-16.

He recalls: "My wife Barbara and Alex's wife Lynn were talking backstage towards the end of the final at 16-16 because they simply couldn't bear to watch.

"And apparently this cake got wheeled in towards his dressing room saying something like 'Congratulations Alex "Hurricane" Higgins, world champion 1980'. So Barbara asks 'what's this?' with the match still going on!

"Anyways, when we went for dinner over at a casino afterwards the cake made it over there and I rubbed it all over my face.

"Listen, I know in the Superbowl or the World Series everyone has these caps and T-shirts ready in case they win, but you have to keep it secret until you win!

"I was having a bath the following morning and I realised that it all started all over again, I was world champion but there were exhibitions to do around the UK and my wife and I couldn't go home for a month and the trophy stayed pretty much in the trunk of the car!

"Now you see winners taking it to football stadiums and charity events, but at the time I felt that was rubbing people's faces in it.

"On the overseas champion thing, I always felt like I had a Canadian flag stamped on my forehead wherever I went, everyone knew that about me.

"But I also felt accepted in the UK, maybe treated as an honorary Brit in most places and got treated very well by the fans and the press guys.

"Maybe not so much at the time as I just felt part of a family, but in later years I became aware that it gave other overseas players hope – if Cliff can do it, maybe we can as well.

"Kirk Stevens was one of those that was inspired a bit from Canada, and if he hadn't enjoyed his life quite as much maybe he could have done the same."

Chapter 3

Steve Davis v Tony Knowles, 1982, first round

"I went to the nightclub, Josephine's, and didn't get back until about 4am – it relaxed me, I didn't get drunk, I was just winding down and it helped me take my mind off things"

B Y the time the 1982 World Championship came around, the era of Steve Davis had most certainly taken hold. The previous year Davis, the boy from Plumstead in south-east London who had teamed up with accountant, businessman and would-be promoter Barry Hearn in Romford, had realised his dream by winning a first world title at the Crucible.

The plan for world domination, hatched in Essex in 1978, had yielded a first dividend in spectacular style 12 months earlier when the Nugget, as he was known to a fiercely partisan army of Romford supporters not least for his ability to make them a lot of money with the bookmakers, held the trophy aloft following an 18-12 victory over Welshman Doug Mountjoy in the final.

And the images of the ebullient Hearn almost knocking him over after the final ball was potted with a part rugby tackle, part bear hug were all still fresh in the memory.

Davis, now 24, had raised the bar in terms of dedication and commitment to his sport and was a hot favourite to follow up with a second successive triumph in Sheffield. And there was nothing in the way the season had panned out to suggest that he would not take care of first-round opponent Tony Knowles.

Knowles, a 26-year-old from Bolton, was a two-time winner of the UK Junior Championship and had crossed swords with Davis many times in those early days. He had also had to fight hard to gain admission to the professional ranks, having twice been rejected by the WPBSA.

Knowles' natural game was expansive, attacking and high-scoring, and though talented no one seriously expected the 150-1 shot for the title to stand up to the matchplay of Davis in a best-of-19-frame match.

And in those days the now-famous 'Crucible Curse', that has at the time of writing still not seen a first-time winner of the World Championship successfully defend their title, had yet to enter into the public consciousness.

Davis had already won six titles that season, and been runner-up in three more, merely confirming that he was going to be the man to beat once again – while Knowles had not featured in a final.

However, the one thing Knowles did not lack, at least on the outside, was confidence and he approached that first evening session on 30 April with little trepidation.

Knowles says: "I may have been an outsider, but had an even money bet with a friend of mine on the match for £150, which was a lot of money in them days.

"He owned a nightclub in Prestwich, and the week before Bryan Robson and Terry McDermott had been in that club and joked that I would be beaten by Steve and back there soon!

"But I was full of confidence, because I thought I could beat him at his own game – that was my philosophy, even though I was usually an attacking player.

"You might think that Steve came in very confident but I don't think he was that year. He had played me a couple of times before, and I could have beaten him at Pontins.

"And another time at the Scottish Masters I could have beaten him too, you remember these things even after 30 to 35 years.

"Steve as everyone knows is a lot of fun these days and outgoing – but back then he was snooker, snooker, snooker. He played a controlled game, that's why he dominated.

"And he adapted it for the length of match, he played the right shot to win. Me, Jimmy White and Alex Higgins had a wider variety of shots, due to playing more exhibitions and entertaining.

"I have seen the same thing with Ronnie O'Sullivan in the past couple of years, difficulties getting back into the matchplay mould after playing so many exhibitions.

"I grew up with Steve as amateurs, that's one reason why I wasn't scared of him. Some of the older players were afraid of this new kid on the block."

Strangely the unease that Knowles had sensed in his opponent was confirmed by Davis. Despite being the defending champion and the dominant player during the 1981–82 season, this was new and uncharted territory – with expectations and pressures the likes of which Davis had not previously experienced.

Davis hoped he had not done too much exhibition, promotional and commercial work in the build-up, but essentially his preparations were normal, and as they always had been for the World Championship.

Davis says: "It was uncharted territory, because even though you had scaled the peak and won the world title the year before, nothing could prepare you for that year.

"Every tournament you were announced as world champion there was a great buzz, and there was an air of expectation on my performance now.

41

"Mainly I was delivering on that in the 1981–82 season but I did lose 5-0 to Ray Reardon in Scotland and I was just feeling the heat a bit in the build-up to the Crucible.

"I didn't have the experience of that, defending, it is different – and that probably is why the Crucible Curse, that no first-time winner has defended there, has lasted so long.

"And maybe that loss to Tony perhaps set the tone for the Curse a bit, because I would have been one of those you might have expected to have a go at defending.

"You're not playing against people that are rubbish, and if you give them breathing space they can play.

"I knew Tony was a very good and talented player and a great cueist, and also a great front-runner. In the past I hadn't had many problems with him, not on raw talent, but just on matchplay.

"But on any given day if your matchplay is not up to scratch someone can pick the pieces up.

"I had started to lose my form in the months before, and though my routine and practice was the same, in between other work, I didn't feel totally at ease."

The match started at 7.30pm, and Knowles executed his pre-match plan to perfection – to forsake his normal positive approach, and take Davis on at his own game. That involved leaving him nothing easy to go for, keeping a tight control of the table, and waiting for mistakes. This was a risky strategy in many ways, since mistakes were not Davis's stock in trade – but it worked.

And a combination of Knowles taking huge glee in his front-running exploits, and Davis being simply unable to haul himself out of a miserable abyss of pressure, helped set up one of if not the greatest shocks in Crucible history.

Knowles surged into a 4-0 lead, even though his highest break in that streak was just 39. And though Davis pulled one back further breaks of 67, 55, 34 and 43 saw Knowles finish 8-1 up overnight. The match was effectively over.

Knowles adds: "Steve's highest break was only 32 in that match, and there was a reason for that. My plan was to control him.

"Steve was very good at coming from behind to win frames, and clearing the least few reds and colours – and often didn't make the early part of the running.

"And I resolved to try and keep him behind the green spot, and didn't play my normal open game but closed it all down.

"It took discipline to do that for me, but the goal was to win the match. It was different then, more of a chess game for most players, nowadays most of them attack more.

"You manipulated the balls to break an opening from your opponent. So I wanted him tied up, and the longer it went on the more frustrated he got.

"I was a big break-builder and heavy scorer by nature, so it was a struggle to play this way but I thought it gave me my best chance."

However, the night was not yet over for Knowles, who despite being back on the table in the morning with the greatest victory of his career so close, headed off in characteristically hedonistic fashion to Josephine's nightclub, the celebrity hangout of choice in the Steel City for almost 40 years, until the small hours.

He says: "I had got off to a flier, going 4-0 up, then 8-1 after the first session overnight – and then came back to win the next two in the morning without hardly a wink of sleep.

"I think it was about two hours, we started on the Friday night and came back for 10.45am on the Saturday morning.

"But I went to the nightclub, Josephine's, and didn't get back until about 4am, before being back on the table early.

"It relaxed me, I didn't get drunk, I was just winding down and it helped me take my mind off things. Would it have been better to go to the hotel room and think about it all? Not for me.

"I enjoyed it, and took it all in, did what I would normally do to relax. I think Steve had arcade games installed in his room that year, Pacman or Space Invaders or something – that's what he did, knocking out little white men going across a screen. But this is what I did.

"Andrew 'Chubby' Chandler who manages the golfers was there supporting me for that match, it must have been one of his first visits to the Crucible."

Davis was simply unable to shake off the bad vibes he had felt before the match, or alter the course of the contest once things started to go wrong. The loss to Knowles was to provide him with one of the most humbling and traumatic defeats of his career, but also the motivation and spur to make sure similar collapses never happened again.

And Davis also admits that despite having never used a sports psychologist throughout his career, he could have done with assistance of that nature against Knowles, trapped in a vortex of gloom about the way things were panning out while his opponent was twirling his cue around his fingers, as in exhibitions, like a cheerleader's baton to the delight of the crowd.

Davis reflects: "It was a funny thing with me, I never liked any other professional watching me practising, and certainly not waiting, hovering to get on after you.

"And I remember that day I had spread balls across the middle of the table and was trying to pot them in the corners.

"Willie Thorne was watching me, and I got about 12 out of 21, anything over half was okay – and he said 'You're cueing great' as an aside.

"But when I went out the first frame went wrong and I just collapsed. My highest break was 30-something, 32 I think.

"And that's the thing about the Crucible, I have had both sides of it. You can feel there is nowhere else you'd rather be on the planet, and you are playing the best snooker.

"But especially in the first round you can feel you can hardly let the cue go, the arm is so tight. And on that occasion I seized up, my ability couldn't overcome the pressure and expectation.

"I felt all the eyes on me, it was starting to go wrong and the hole got deeper – and I couldn't get out of it.

"The intimate nature of the place means it can be tough to turn it around if you are having a bad day. The next year I was a different animal, expectation was more sensible. Having not defended I was going out to get them again, rather than them trying to get me.

"But I have had scares in the first round and gone on to win the title. John Virgo and Neal Foulds spring to mind, 10-8s, too close for comfort. I have never had a sports psychologist in my corner but you can look at certain times and think, 'One might have been useful then.' And I think that about this match.

"Maybe they could have spotted a trend in what was happening, because this was one where I let the outside world in to mess up my usual positive thinking.

"The first frame changed everything for me, it was that fragile that day. I needed to think at 4-0 down, 'We've been here before, let's pull this round,' but I didn't in that match.

"I didn't make it hard for him, got bad vibes about the day, sensed the glee in the crowd that they were loving it and I didn't like that – and ended up playing the part and succumbing.

"I felt as if it was what they wanted, and I wasn't strong, stroppy or thick-skinned enough to change things.

"I was never great coming from behind – most of the time I wasn't behind, in fairness. Being behind by that far was a shock to the system.

"The thing about Tony Knowles was he had a bit of swagger and was a bit of a show-off around the table when he was in front.

"He played this massé shot to get out of a snooker and then did this thing he did, twirling his cue around his fingers like a cheerleader's baton as if in an exhibition.

"And when I saw him doing it I just thought, 'I'm bang in trouble here, if he is enjoying it that much.'

"Normally it might make a player angry that he was doing that, or had been in a nightclub all night, but it all just made the hole deeper.

"I am inhibited and playing rubbish, he is playing great, he has the bravado to act like that and the crowd were loving it. It all just added to the woes. I stayed in Sheffield for a few days and went on a total bender."

Hearn was as shocked as Davis, and was not about to let him forget what had happened in a hurry – reasoning that his player would be so hurt by what had taken place that efforts would be redoubled on the practice table ahead of the 1983 World Championship.

He says: "We were so confident before that match. I had shipped up a load of amusement arcade games for Steve, we had a suite at the Grosvenor House, everything logistically was ticked. But he went out that day and didn't play, and Tony played out of his skull.

"We went back to the hotel that first night, with Steve 8-1 down, and over a meal I said to the waitress, 'Bring us two bottles of champagne.'

"Steve looked at me and said 'Why, what are we celebrating? And I said to him, 'That's as close as you are going to get to it this year, so we'll have a bit now.'

"We sat there after in the dressing room, and that was a year virtually all my players, who were becoming the Matchroom Mob, got knocked out in the first round.

"And I told Steve we would throw a huge 'Losers' Party' back in Romford because I knew he wouldn't like that. We had our Winners' Parties, and this was a huge one – all about losing.

"I wanted it to be right out there, he got slaughtered by Tony, he was a loser and that got into his head and stayed there all year because he hated losing – with a few reminders from me.

"And it was a motivator for him. It was one of the biggest upsets in the history of the Crucible. Steve had hardly lost all season, and was odds-on for the title with the bookies. As long as you learn from the bad defeats, losing can make you stronger."

Despite his lack of sleep Knowles had quickly taken the two frames he needed on the Saturday morning to seal a famous shock victory, one that blew the tournament wide open. He was to reach the semi-finals at the Crucible on three occasions later in his career, but was denied a place in the final four this year after a spectacular meltdown against Australia's Eddie Charlton, losing the last seven frames from 11-6 up to go down 13-11 in the quarter-finals.

In later years Knowles, living up to his 'Bolton Stud' sobriquet, was to become almost as well-known for his sexual conquests off the table, so often plastered over the front pages of red-top newspapers, as for his feats on it. One particularly lurid set of revelations saw him fined £5,000 by the WPBSA for bringing the game into disrepute.

But he remained one of the huge characters in snooker's boom-time, and two of his three semi-final Crucible defeats – in 1985 and 1986 – were to eventual winners Dennis Taylor and Joe Johnson, both of whom he would have been seeded to beat.

Knowles, who won two ranking events in his career, adds: "Later that tournament I got to the quarters and lost the last seven frames against Eddie Charlton to go down 13-11. I just fell apart.

"It was new to me and I didn't cope and panicked, it was a lack of experience. I should have turned Eddie over easily, but he was very clever.

"I am a little disappointed that I didn't win more, given the qualities and technical ability I had. I missed a chance of winning the World Championship in 1983, losing to Cliff 16-15 in the semi-final.

"I think I should have won it that year, and I won a great quarter-final against Jimmy White in 1985 before losing to Dennis Taylor in the semi-final, and we know what happened that year.

"And then I lost to Joe Johnson in the semis the following year, who also went on to win a first world title. I was seeded to beat both of them. But I wasn't playing well at that time because I had been hounded by the press for a couple of years and my game had suffered, trying to prove something.

"It was hard to snap out of it. I had become one of the main talking points, a bit like Ronnie O'Sullivan has had to put up with.

"It was different then – people believed what was written in the papers! But they shouldn't have done.

"There was an article in 1984 when I was on about 11 pages, the front page for five days in a row or something daft.

"I think I would have got to No.1 if I had beaten John Parrott in the first round in 1984, but I had all this coverage for days and I fell apart basically.

"It was an article that got out of control, and everything went wild. I'm not sure there has ever been another sportsman on the front page for five days in a row."

But it was the back pages that Knowles made with this famous victory, and the Crucible Curse was born.

Chapter 4

Alex Higgins v Jimmy White, 1982, semi-final

"Geniuses are born for moments – it isn't the way you would coach someone, but they are born to leave a mark on this planet and in this break it was something outside of Alex that made it happen"

IT looked a treat on paper, and it delivered in almost every respect – a semi-final World Championship match-up between the undisputed People's Champion Alex 'Hurricane' Higgins, and his heir apparent, the youthful and hugely talented Jimmy 'Whirlwind' White.

Most great Crucible matches carry a calling-card, and for this one it was to prove a break of 69 from Higgins at a crucial stage of the contest, a backs-to-the-wall, death or glory tour de force that would swiftly enter into snooker folklore.

Higgins, already featured earlier in these pages, was again bidding for a second world title now ten years after his first, and attempting to take advantage of the absence of pre-tournament favourite Steve Davis in the latter stages of the Crucible draw. And the callow youth White, just 20, was only just embarking on a career that seemed certain at that time to yield one or more world titles along the way, such was his frightening natural ability.

These two players were no mere winning machines, both had the desire to entertain and perform in their sporting DNA, inspiring a love from fans that arguably Stephen Hendry, for all his greatness, never fully experienced and possibly Steve Davis not until his later years and his transformation from 'Nugget' to 'national treasure'.

Left-hander White had won the English Amateur Championship in 1979, and the World Amateur a year later, the perfect springboard and platform to turning professional in 1980.

Born in Tooting and falling all too easily into some kind of 'Artful Dodger' stereotype, White may have looked, talked and acted like a south London ducker and diver, but on the table he was fearless and put huge doubt in the minds of his more experienced opponents.

All of a sudden some of their traditional containing strategies appeared inadequate – nothing was safe, the kid could pot anything, seemingly from anywhere, and was capable of making the cue ball do things that were unheard of outside, and even during, exhibition routines.

In only a second season as a pro White had won two titles, beating Cliff Thorburn 9-4 to win the Scottish Masters, and Steve Davis 11-9 to win the Northern Ireland Classic. These were two huge, morale-boosting milepost successes for the Whirlwind, giving him plenty of confidence coming in to his second World Championship.

In 1981 he had lost a superb first-round match with Steve Davis, this year he had come past Thorburn, South Africa's Perrie Mans, and then another Canadian Kirk Stevens in the quarter-finals.

Higgins had lost to Davis in 1981 after his final loss to Thorburn in 1980, and for many the likelihood of him ever repeating his 1972 glories was fading fast.

This year, in a season where he had not won a title and was by his own admission concerned about his form heading for Sheffield, he beat Jim Meadowcroft 10-5 in the first round, followed that up with a nerve-shredding 13-12 win over Wales's Doug Mountjoy in the last 16, and then set up the clash with White by seeing off Willie Thorne 13-10 in the quarter-finals.

For White, this was his first match at the Crucible against the player he revered above all others, and quite apart from the enjoyment it offered to those among the audience and the millions of TV viewers, a moment to be cherished and savoured – win or lose.

He says: "First and foremost, when I was about 11 and started to find snooker from pool I remember watching Alex Higgins play a shot on *Pot Black*.

"There was a black over the middle pocket and he potted it off two cushions with check side when there was a much easier way to pot it.

"And really from that moment, whether consciously or subconsciously, my career became about entertaining myself and the public. He was a massive influence on me, like seeing George Best or Lionel Messi with the ball at their feet, you couldn't wait to see what they would do next.

"You don't get that often in sport, and Ronnie O'Sullivan has been another for us in snooker. He is special to watch, but Alex was my hero.

"I had played him before but all of a sudden here I was playing my idol in the semi-finals of the World Championship. Just to be playing him there, I was in my element.

"Obviously winning would have been the icing on the cake, but I was playing my hero, it was a dream playing Alex at the Crucible.

"I had won the World Amateur and the English Amateur, but this was the biggest match of my life up to that point.

"Snooker was lucky to find that place for its World Championship and the electricity in there could be amazing. When it's down the one table like that, you can hear a pin drop. Then when the excitement levels go up, if you're focused, you hear nothing, if you are not, you hear everything."

Watching the 30th frame and Higgins' famous break back again, as I and so many others have done countless times, it becomes almost more unbelievable with every viewing. Jack Karnehm and John Spencer were in the commentary box for the BBC, and with White at the table and in full flow the former world champion observed: "And you get the feeling this could be the winning break."

Even when White missed a relatively straightforward red, a lead of 59-0 looked likely to see him over the line to a 16-14 victory and into a first World Championship final.

Instead, something extraordinary happened, the kind of feat under the most intense pressure that only very few sportspeople can produce.

With six reds left and a possible 75 points on the table the chance was there for Higgins, but one red was nastily placed on the side cushion near the yellow spot, and the black was up near the baulk colours.

But the fact that Higgins so often seemed to be out of position, requiring yet another brilliant recovery pot time after time after time, only added to the drama.

Higgins was exasperated after potting the first, simple red, left leaning against the table after leaving himself without any clear shot on a colour when that should not have been an issue.

After much deliberation he took on a long green into its own pocket, taking an early opportunity to develop the most difficult of the reds into a slightly more favourable position. There were still plenty enough points to play with.

Sensing this was a huge moment in not only the match, but also his career and life, Higgins was if anything even more animated than usual as he prowled around the table.

A thin cut on the next red sent the cue call careering up the table towards the baulk end, coming to rest close to the yellow.

But another low percentage shot was on, a long black to get the highest value colour back on its spot, and it duly disappeared. The player allowed himself a smile to the audience.

As ever Higgins was twitching, up on his shots, but there had never been any question about his shot-making ability and it was this that he most needed to come to the fore. It did not let him down.

There was another thin cut on the partially developed red into the centre pocket, again without total control of the cue ball leaving him with a tough blue – but there was little doubt Higgins was going to take it on, and the force was with him by now.

There was another pause for thought, or possibly for dramatic effect. The break was only 13 at this stage but it felt like much more already and as Karnehm observed: "Alex knows he cannot afford any mistakes, he must get a colour or it could be the end of the match."

Another brilliant, odds-against shot on the blue was played with so much side that the white sped off the side cushion before coming to rest adjacent to the black.

There were only difficult long reds to choose from with now three left on the table, and after Higgins knocked a great pot into the green pocket he now had for the first time something approaching control of the table, finishing well on the black.

"I'm feeling nervous for him," intoned Spencer. "If he clears this, it would be the break of the tournament."

Higgins comfortably potted that black and added two more from the remaining two reds, and with the colours now on their spots was favourite to take the match into a deciding 31st frame. But there was still the little matter of the pressure to deal with, and he needed all of them.

However there were going to be no mistakes from here for Higgins, this was the kind of moment and memory he was born to provide. The yellow, green and brown were followed by the blue, he rolled the cue ball through potting the pink, and the black made it a frame-winning clearance of 69 and brought the house down at the Crucible.

With White sitting in his chair looking shell-shocked, Higgins sauntered back to his own seat on the other side of the arena and looked up at the commentary box, winking and pointing his index finger to the sky.

Whether this was meant as 'No.1', or even 'One more frame to go', as he later was to confirm, it matters little. It could have been either. And there would be far worse images to capture the entire appeal of Higgins as a player and performer. Defiant, and drunk on the moment as the love, adulation and appreciation rained down from the seats at the Crucible.

Higgins knew exactly how good what he had done was. With his back against the wall and under the most intense pressure, he had produced his very best.

In his autobiography *My Story*, Higgins said: "Jimmy looked calm and confident. He had strung me along with some great snooker… this youngster I loved like a brother was making me work like a dog. I needed this frame to stay in the contest, the adrenaline was pumping but I play better under pressure. Those money games that I'd been playing over 15 years stood me in good stead.

"I had promised Lauren that Daddy would win the world title that year, and that was one promise I intended to keep.

"I knew I had to clear the table to win. With five points on the board I went for a risky black, I knew it was going to be the shot that determined the rest of the frame.

"There was a slight judder in the jaws of the hole, as the black disappeared into the pocket. What Jimmy was going through was anyone's guess, but there was no room for error and I tried not to think of anything but winning.

"The black went in and the crowd erupted – '69!'. As I walked back to my chair I was totally oblivious of Jimmy. I looked up to the gallery and raised my index finger – 'Just one more'. At the end of the match, in my joy I also felt his disappointment. I was almost sorry I'd beaten him."

Speaking last year about the famous Higgins clearance, Ronnie O'Sullivan said: "It was an incredible match, and an incredible end to the match. Sadly Alex is no longer with us, but he and Jimmy have always been two players I have loved and admired for the way they entertained the fans.

"You had to feel sorry for Jimmy because he had no right to lose that frame at 15-14, and the semi-final as a match. For Higgins to come up with a clearance like that, I can't imagine how he must have felt going in to that final frame.

"You're going to be wondering, 'What am I even doing here playing a decider?' after some of the balls Higgins had potted in the previous frame. And it has been compounded over time because Jimmy has not gone on to win the world title. He could have done it that year.

"But as iconic moments go, I honestly don't think it gets much bigger than what Higgins did that day.

"What it is, I look at it and think only certain characters are born for moments, and he was born to give moments like that. George Best was the same, Maradona, Lionel Messi is like that. They are such geniuses, that although it might not be conventionally the right way to go about things, it isn't the way you would coach someone, they are born to leave their mark on this planet.

"And with that break it was like it was something outside of him that made it happen. Usain Bolt is another one – put on this planet to provide moments that people will remember long after they are gone.

"Jimmy brought that moment out of Alex the way he was playing, though I'm sure he wished he hadn't. You'd have fancied Jimmy against Ray Reardon, though nothing is certain in sport."

It was always going to be difficult for White to regroup in time for the next, decisive 31st frame, though he was in first only to break down on six.

Higgins made a break of 59 that was routine by comparison with what had gone shortly before, only to run out of position and miss a red with still 75 points left on.

White did have another good chance but he looked to be mentally in turmoil and the opportunity came and went, allowing Higgins to close out the victory.

"One of the most exciting matches I have ever seen in my life," said Spencer.

But there was no triumphalism in the face of his beaten opponent this time from Higgins. White was as a little brother to him, someone who shared the same creed about the way snooker should be played, who saw himself as a performer and not just a player, and like Higgins lived to entertain and not just to win.

Alex Higgins v Jimmy White

The crestfallen 20-year-old got a hug, and White was of course to prove a worthy inheritor of the 'People's Champion' mantle in the years to come. Higgins returned to his chair, kissed his baby Lauren's dummy that had been kept with him as a lucky charm, and the smiles represented a deep satisfaction that he had earned another chance of winning that elusive second world title.

White adds: "I was a bit naïve in the match, only just 20. I had a glass of milk, and he started asking me if I had the bottle for this one!

"I had played in snooker halls for years when if you didn't win the match you could literally, physically, get beaten up so I knew what pressure was. But this was different.

"In the second session I was 8-4 up at one stage. And then shortly after, I think at 8-5, he takes on a brown in the green pocket, he misses it by that far that it goes round the table and ends up in the yellow pocket, and finishes on the blue. So that could have been 9-5 rather than 8-6.

"It was 11-11 after the third session, and then at 15-14 to me, one frame away from victory, and after I missed that red with the rest he just produced one of the most amazing clearances that has ever been done in snooker.

"Wherever I go in the world people still show the video, maybe they think I've never seen it before!

"There's a guy I knew, we called him Motoring Martin, who I have spoken to many times since. He was getting Higgins large vodka and oranges all through the match.

"So Higgins had had lots to drink by that stage, but he was the only player who could play brilliantly pissed anyway. I saw it in exhibitions, when he came out of the pub steaming and still produced for the public. It was amazing.

"But genuinely I was also pleased for Higgins despite the defeat, because not for one minute did I think I wouldn't win it the next year or the year after.

"It was a great chance of being the youngest ever world champion. I was a bit naïve in some ways, but sometimes your name is just on the trophy and I think Alex's was that year.

"Alex winning that year helped make snooker what it is. It gave the sport a huge boost. I am not saying a win for me wouldn't have been good, but it was a great story, and as ever he was the first to bring the baby out there after the final. That was unheard of before."

White was already starting to enjoy the life and earnings his prodigious talents had afforded him, and not always in the most positive way. In a reference to the start of the late nights, drinking and gambling that became significant factors in his life, White said in his ITV *Life Stories* programme: "If I had won that match and then the title in 1982, I might have ended up killing myself because of the madness that was going on off the table."

Higgins was of course to go on to win the final against Ray Reardon, triggering those iconic scenes with wife Lynn and baby daughter Lauren in the arena. In a shared family celebration that has now become almost ritualised in sporting circles, Higgins was once again a trailblazer.

His World Championship win in 1982 was hugely popular, all the more so for being unexpected with many having viewed his chances of ever winning the big one again as negligible.

And it will be most remembered for a tearful champion holding his baby daughter – and one amazing break in the match of the tournament.

Chapter 5

Terry Griffiths v Cliff Thorburn, 1983, last 16

"I had a dream just two weeks before that I made a 147 at the Crucible, and so it was a very, very strange feeling when I was actually doing it – I felt as if I had been there before"

PLENTY of great matches have one unique selling point – but the second-round World Championship collision of former world champions, Terry Griffiths and Cliff Thorburn, contained at least two. The first ever 147 maximum break made at the Crucible, and the latest-ever finish to a match there of 3.51am.

Canadian Thorburn, already featured on these pages for his 1980 final victory over fierce adversary Alex Higgins, was on the Crucible charge once again in 1983 after being thumped 10-4 in the first round the previous year by Jimmy White.

Thorburn remained a doughty and popular competitor, and had already beaten Griffiths on his way to a Masters title at the Wembley Conference Centre earlier that year, prevailing 9-7 against Ray

Reardon in the final. But what of Griffiths, the new pride of Wales? In 1979 and aged 31 Griffiths had provided what is still one of the greatest stories in World Championship history, coming through as a qualifier in his rookie year on the professional tour to sweep all before him and lift the trophy with a 24-16 victory over Reardon.

"I'm in the final now, you know," a reaction after beating Eddie Charlton to reach the showpiece and uttered with the characteristic lilting Welsh delivery, became a catchphrase to be repeated endlessly on television in the years that followed.

Born in Llanelli, Griffiths had worked as a miner, postman, bus conductor, and insurance salesman before turning professional in 1978, having by then won both the Welsh and English Amateur Championships.

A cool temperament, laconic manner and dry sense of humour endeared Griffiths to both the public and his fellow players. And while the 1980s will forever be known as the 'Steve Davis years', Griffiths came as close as anyone to threatening that hegemony, certainly in the first five or six years of the decade.

Griffiths always seemed to play the right shot even under the most intense pressure, being blessed with an ice-cool nerve, and knew the game inside out having turned professional with years on the clock on the exhibition circuit.

These qualities were not only to serve him well as a player, but also in later life as a commentator, and also as a coach to younger players. In that forum Griffiths was to really show another side to his abilities, passing on both technical and mental titbits for those smart enough to listen.

Both revelled in their hard-earned reputations for being masters of the tactical side of the game, taking pride in being the one to outlast their opponent in a safety exchange and watching them crack first.

Griffiths had already won the UK Championship that season, beating Alex Higgins 16-15 in a brilliant final, and had beaten Mark Wildman in the first round to set up the clash with Thorburn for a place in the quarter-finals.

It looked a titanic tussle even on paper. Griffiths remembered Thorburn being interviewed about the contest before it had begun: "One of the press guys sat us down together before our last-16 match to do a preview, and I will always remember Cliff saying, in that lovely deep Canadian voice, 'I can tell you this mate – it isn't going to be pretty,'" recalls Griffiths with a smile.

"But we had a good rivalry between us, we were great friends but there was never any quarter asked or given out there. Cliff was one of the great characters of our game, still is, and it was always a pleasure to play against him."

For his part, Thorburn says: "I knew it was going to be a tough game. We were both former world champions, and all my matches with Terry tended to be close."

With no breaks above 39, an effort from Griffiths in frame one, Thorburn led 2-1 after the first three frames with no one realising that history was about to be made. Though Steve Davis had made the first televised maximum 147 break in professional competition in January 1982 at the Lada Classic, winning himself a car, no one had done it on the ultimate proving ground at the Crucible in the World Championship.

Thorburn recalls: "In the first session I didn't feel well at all, I remember that. I had a heavy cold, and had only slept about two hours the night before. It wasn't great preparation for this of all matches. I felt awful.

"But maybe that took my mind off the actual game because there were no nerves, and then of course I made the 147 going into that first interval. I had a dream just two weeks before the Crucible that I made a 147 in the World Championship.

"In the dream I played one shot potting a black, coming off the top cushion and splitting the reds perfectly.

"So it was a very, very strange feeling when I was actually doing it – I felt as if I had been there before, even though no one had ever done it at the Crucible. Maybe that's how I stayed calm.

"And a year previous to that I had a dream about golf, where I was talking to Jack Nicklaus for about four hours. I mentioned this to a friend while we were playing at one of the Surrey courses, and I shot a 68 – to this day my best ever round.

"So I was in the habit of people looking at me, raising an eyebrow and asking, 'Any dreams last night, Cliff?'"

As Griffiths broke off in frame four, Thorburn had claimed a narrow 2-1 lead but there had been no breaks of significance to that point.

After a short tactical exchange the Welshman fouled attempting to roll up to a red on the top cushion.

That left the Canadian with a straight-ish opener, but despite missing it badly, the red came back off the jaws almost along the top cushion, knocking in another red.

"Well, that's one way of getting them I suppose," said BBC commentator Jack Karnehm. "On the black as well...my word that's a bonus." And it was to prove one of the most famous flukes in history.

With the reds spread these days you might have heard reference made to a possible 147 straight away from commentators Karnehm and Rex Williams, but these were different times, and the feat retained far more of a mystical aura.

There were few problems initially. On 56 Thorburn left himself a tricky red with the rest, having to take care not to touch the blue, but it was executed to perfection, stunning off the side cushion to stay on the black.

"This will be the eighth black," intoned Williams. "Cliff's main objective will be to win the frame but he will certainly be looking for a very big break here, and will be happier and can relax when the frame is safe because there is a great opportunity here."

Karnehm then talked about a high-break prize of £3,000, but the 147 maximum still did not dare speak its name until Williams broached it a pot later. "I'm going to let him finish this one Rex – I'm a wee bit superstitious," said Karnehm.

In the arena Thorburn still seemed calm and very much in his routine as he manipulated the white ball around the black and remaining reds.

Griffiths, for his part, had clearly dealt with losing the frame and was sitting in his chair with a smile on his face, willing his rival and opponent on to a piece of Crucible history.

A round of applause broke out as Thorburn potted the 13th black to bring up the century, but standing on 104 with two reds left he was not done yet.

With the tension rising and Thorburn worrying about how to pot black No.14 while getting the right position on the final red, he returned to his seat announcing, "I might have a little break here," to applause from the audience as he blew his nose and wiped down his cue and sweaty palms.

"What a moment, it is truly electric here," confirmed Karnehm. As Thorburn addressed the final red play had stopped on the other table in the match featuring Thorburn's fellow Canadian Bill Werbeniuk, and David Taylor.

Thorburn left himself a testing yellow, but that smacked against the back of the pocket, and as he got down to the black, for a total of £18,000, Karnehm famously whispered "Good luck, mate".

But there was no luck needed as the 16th black went down and Thorburn, drained, sank to his knees next to the table and punched the air, before shaking the hand of referee John Williams and sharing a three-way hug with Griffiths and Werbeniuk, who had been following the break by peering around the partition.

The crowd gave Thorburn a prolonged standing ovation – but once the clamour had died down he was still only 3-1 up in a best-of-25-frame match, and there was still a long way to go. A very long way, as it turned out.

Griffiths says: "Of course the early match was dominated by the 147 in the fourth frame from Cliff, the first one ever at the Crucible after that fluked red.

"And that is something I was very proud to have been a part of really, it was something very special and to be out there watching it in the best seat was tremendous."

As it turned out, there was not only the task of calming himself down and re-focusing on the remainder of the match after such a huge high to deal with but some altogether more tragic and personal news to process for Thorburn, something that came to light as he walked off the table leading 4-3 following the first session.

"I can still see myself leaving the venue with my package of Embassy cigarettes in my hand, holding them up and very happy," says Thorburn.

"Then when the session was over and Terry had won the last two to be 4-3 only behind I phoned my wife, who was pregnant. But when I did she just said, 'I am so sorry for losing the baby at four months.' I didn't even know about it, I had no idea.

"A couple of good friends had found out the day before but didn't think they should tell me before the match. So you're getting loads of people putting cameras in your face after this 147 and saying 'Come on Cliff, smile', and 'Don't you ever smile?' And I am hearing this on the phone, it was brutal and smiling was the last thing I wanted to do.

"I wanted to come home straight away but Barbara reassured me and told me to stick it out, that her mum and sister were there, and that she was okay."

Thorburn manfully played on despite the turmoil and extreme emotions running amok inside his head. He kept Griffiths at bay in the second session, taking an 8-6 lead into the concluding frames. By this time the pair had only completed 14 frames, leaving a possible 15 still to play. They were to need all of them.

And to make matters worse, the rule calling for players to come off the table in their final session if over the allotted time had not yet been brought in. This meant that the match on the same table between Eddie Charlton and John Spencer, another epic, was allowed to finish before Thorburn and Griffiths were allowed back on in the evening.

The final session therefore did not start until around 9.30pm and Charlton's 13-11 victory secured, with still a very long way to go. The rules were subsequently changed as a direct result of this match.

Thorburn edged ahead to 12-9, only for Griffiths to roar back, a break of 97 tying the scores up at 12-12 and forcing a deciding frame.

Griffiths says: "Late? It wasn't that late a finish, what's wrong with people! My dad did say something to me at the end of the match, the sort of thing that only dads can say to you.

"I had lost 13-12 at ten to four in the morning or whenever it was. My dad generally was a man of few words about snooker, and said very little to me about my game.

"It was usually just 'Well, you didn't play too well today boy', or 'You played pretty good today, boy' – and that was about it.

"But this time he said to me, 'You know if he hadn't have fluked that red in the fourth frame, you'd have won the match 13-12!' That was a long way to look back in a best-of-25-frame match!

"They hadn't brought the rule in yet about pulling players off the table in a final session if they had gone on beyond their time.

"So there was this other second-round match on our table between Eddie Charlton and John Spencer, and we didn't get to start the final session until 9.15pm or 9.30pm instead of at 7pm.

"That was the reason that they ended up changing that rule, because there was something like 1,000 people in the foyer trying to get in for our game, and it was chaos because the arena was full of people watching the other one.

"Charlton was about 12-7 ahead and then Spencer kept coming back to 12-11 before it finally finished 13-11 to Eddie. It just took forever.

"We had only got seven frames played in our first session, that was quite good for us two. But now here we were coming back at 9.15pm with still a possible 11 frames to play, and as it turned out we needed all of them. It went to the wire.

"I was 12-9 down at one point and I won the next three frames, they were hard frames and really he should have won the match during those.

"So I thought I had him, but he went out for a break, came back, and then made a 75 to win the match – I was devastated.

"To be honest I wasn't sure how many people were still there, just the ones that were about five yards away in the front couple of rows, after that I was blind!

"I think I must have had about 14 hot chocolates in that game. There were some BBC staff, some WPBSA staff still around. We all know how it goes with these late finishes. You think 'It won't be long now', and then it just goes on and on.

"Look, there might have been 100 left in the crowd and to be fair we did all we could to get rid of them in that match. We are talking real die-hards.

"Nobody has a joke with me when I have lost 13-12 in the World Championship, so there was none of that. I would have killed them!

"But that was two pretty big things in that match – the first ever 147 at the Crucible, and the latest ever finish at the venue.

"There weren't too any matches involving Cliff and myself that you would have called memorable. We were just two dogged old guys that never, ever gave up and the matches often went like this. The safety play was of high quality, and the potting wasn't."

For Thorburn, the memories were of how hard it had been to get any kind of meal on a Sunday night going in to Monday morning, and how Willie Thorne – possibly with a financial interest in the outcome – was one of those to stick it out until the small-hours finish.

"I had been 12-9 up but Terry won three in a row, ending up with a break of 97 to make it 12-12 so he was feeling good at that point," he says.

"Of course we didn't start that final session until very late, I think it was around 9.30pm, while the Eddie Charlton and John Spencer match finished on our table.

"To be honest if there were two players a 4am finish wasn't going to bother too much, that was Terry and I.

"The average frame time back then probably was around half an hour. People always seemed to want to beat me in safety and tactical exchanges, I honestly don't know why they bothered. It's what I wanted them to do.

"Terry had a great safety game, Dennis Taylor too, Steve Davis of course, Alex Higgins, but you were trying not to give the other guy anything to shoot. And don't think it was always fun being me out there, it wasn't.

"I stuck with it, this was the World Championship and I vaguely remember there still being about 200 people at 3.30am.

"Willie Thorne was there and Racing Raymond, his great racing friend. They may have had a punt or two on it."

"After I won and it was finally all done you do all the usual stuff with any media, and of course I was exhausted, I felt like I had been out drinking all night.

"It was a Sunday night, or rather a Monday morning, and it was hard enough back then to get a meal normally on a Sunday night.

"No meal at the hotel, I do remember it was very hard to get food before and during the match.

"I think it was getting towards dawn by the time we left the building, maybe some milk wagons around. I certainly hadn't got to sleep before the sun came up, and I maybe got about two hours' rest.

"I felt like Fast Eddie did after beating Minnesota Fats in their first pool session. Terry was a very civilised character – he liked his tea and biscuits while he was playing, dunking his cookies in, that is how he relaxed."

As players, officials and spectators stumbled out of the building dodging milk floats in their bleary-eyed state the sun was coming up, and a new week beginning in Sheffield.

But the reverberations from this particular match would continue to be felt for some time. Only the second 147 ever made on television, it brought both Thorburn and the sport worldwide attention.

Grateful staff at the BBC acknowledged what Thorburn had done for their coverage, but although the tough-as-teak Canadian somehow and miraculously scrapped his way into another World Championship final, two further final-frame victories over Kirk Stevens and Tony Knowles after what had gone before left him with almost nothing in the tank for another encounter with Steve Davis, and he went down 18-6.

"Nick Hunter, the BBC producer, had really wanted to have someone make a 147 at the Crucible and the World Championship," Thorburn says. "They had been talking it up a bit, and when I did make it a bunch of the film crew gave me some silver cufflinks and three wine chalices with my wife's name and my only son at the time on there. I treasure those, because they were from the heart.

"They were so pleased someone had done it, and I was the lucky one. It is the perfect place to do it, and a lot of people still say they remember watching it or reading about it. I have probably had about 10,000 people say to me they were in the arena.

"I was pretty drained after the Terry match and the news from home. There was another very tough match against Kirk Stevens, that I won 13-12. And then yet another deciding frame in the semi-final against Tony Knowles, that one finished 16-15.

"I am not saying Steve Davis wouldn't have beaten me anyway, but there really wasn't much left in the tank and he beat me easily 18-6 in the final."

There were two other memories of the momentous first Crucible 147 that have stuck with Thorburn, one very uplifting, another not so edifying. He recalls: "I was supposed to get £3,000 for the high break, £10,000 for the 147, and £5,000 for the new championship high break, or £18,000 – plus the £15,000 for finishing as runner-up, a total of £33,000.

"But the cheque I got was for £28,000. So I queried this with the WPBSA, who said I didn't get the new championship high-break record. I asked why not, as it had been paid to Doug Mountjoy previously. And they said that's just the way it is, and we can't really have you getting more than the overall winner! Steve Davis got £30,000 for winning.

"I have to be honest that is still a slight bone of contention with me, just the 33 years that has irritated me. There wasn't anything in writing, but it did change my opinion of a few people. I hope it isn't sour grapes, but if you are promised something, you should get it."

Far more enjoyable was an experience at the Olympic Stadium in Montreal for an Expos baseball game, when the final few shots of Thorburn's Crucible 147 were played on the Jumbatron video screen between innings. Thorburn described it as "one of the best moments of my life – I have a great photo of that scoreboard taken by one of my brothers-in-law."

Chapter 6

Steve Davis v Dennis Taylor, 1985, final

*"You can't lose if you're Steve in that match –
you are 8-0 up against Dennis Taylor and you
cannot lose, it is absolutely impossible"*

LEAVING other matches out of this book may cause irritation or bewilderment. Leaving the 1985 World Championship final out might have provoked a riot, and a contest that has long since entered into sporting iconography had to be in football-speak the 'first name on the team-sheet'.

The mid-1980s were troubling times in Great Britain, a country that not only seemed ill at ease, but openly at war with itself throughout the miners' strike of 1984–85, and via a football hooliganism problem that was spiralling out of control.

But against this disturbing backdrop the 'gentlemen's' sport of snooker was experiencing a huge domestic boom, a surge in popularity that arguably reached its zenith on the night of Sunday, 28 April 1985 when Dennis Taylor rolled it all into one against

Steve Davis, already a three-time and defending world champion and dominant force – huge shock, magnificent comeback, and most dramatic conclusion.

The black-ball final, as it swiftly came to be known, kept 18.5 million people glued to their television sets until 12.19am and the conclusion of a truly epic battle royal, prompting some never-to-be-forgotten scenes and celebrations – plenty more of which later.

But the seeds for the eventual seismic outcome, as much as for any other match in this collection, were sown earlier in the season.

Northern Irishman Taylor, born in Coalisland, County Tyrone, was 36 by the time of the 1985 World Championship and had previously lost one world final at the Crucible to Terry Griffiths in 1979, a defeat that still haunted him, and an opportunity that he felt strongly he had let slip away.

Taylor was regarded as a brave and canny player if not one to have yet hit the greatest heights in the game. However, his personal and professional worlds were turned upside down in the autumn of 1984, when his mother Annie died unexpectedly at the age of 62. It was a huge shock for Taylor and his family, seeing him pull out of the Jameson International and temporarily at least lose all interest in snooker.

But once persuaded to rejoin the fray at the Grand Prix Taylor was a different animal, almost a man on a mission to pay a proper tribute to his mother. He won a first ranking title with a startling burst of form, claiming an unlikely 10-2 win over Cliff Thorburn in the final.

Taylor says: "My mother's death had a huge impact on me personally, and it came at a time when I had started to play some of the best snooker of my career.

"She was only 62, it was a huge shock and I lost all interest in snooker. It was my family that persuaded me I should get back playing and return at the Grand Prix in her memory.

"That's what I did and the snooker I played there was the best of my life. I was finally getting used to the upside-down glasses designed and made by Jack Karnehm. With them, I am sure I would have beaten Terry Griffiths in the 1979 world final. They made a huge difference.

"I won the Grand Prix beating Cliff 10-2 in the final, almost on a mission, playing for my mum – and that mindset continued through to April and the World Championship.

"Then at the Crucible I won with plenty in hand in the quarters against Cliff, and again in the semis with a session to spare against Tony Knowles.

"So I had got through to the final with something left in the tank, I thought, having had a few sessions off because it is a long haul."

"Steve had given me a few right pastings but I had played okay against him at the Crucible, he had beaten me in the semis and I beat him in 1979 when Barry Hearn was sure he would storm through the field. I had played good snooker against him.

"So I wasn't overawed by him before the match despite the dominance he was exerting on the sport, and I was really up for it."

Davis, now 27, arrived in Sheffield as once again the man to beat and expecting to win a third world title in a row, having lifted the trophy in 1983 and 1984 to add to his 1981 success.

He says: "I came in as world No.1 and favourite for the title, but also my stock had risen. It was obvious that after winning a third world title, it had got in the head of certain players.

"Doug Mountjoy had said in public that I was two blacks better than everyone else, the way we would handicap in clubs – seven points start, 14 points, 21 and so on, and other players weren't too happy he had said it.

"It did feel like others were struggling to play against me, like I had a force field around me and people weren't playing well against me. You sensed sometimes that players had checked out of hotels before they played you, it made you feel almost invincible.

"The team around me was strong, and my matchplay was also strong, as I tried to take the game to another level. I was trying to be more relentless than any player ever seen, and I was capable of winning by huge margins, rather than letting them back into it.

"Dennis had played some good snooker that season, some of the best being played at times. He won the Grand Prix, a first ranking title and he had been like a man on a mission in that event after the very sad loss of his mother earlier in the year.

"He was very clever and canny, underrated as a player, and had worked on his cue action to make it smoother and stop it being so jerky. But he had grit and bottle, and was a streetfighter. But I had given him so many heavy defeats as a pro that I couldn't have been in a better frame of mind."

John Virgo had been working overtime at the 1985 World Championship with his exhibition 'filler' routine, with both semi-finals finishing with a session to spare, and the quarter-finals involving Davis and Taylor also proving to be one-sided affairs against Terry Griffiths and Thorburn respectively.

And it looked in the early stages of the final as if another mismatch was under way, as Davis won all seven of the frames in the first session on the Saturday afternoon, before adding the first of the evening to lead 8-0.

And it was in frame nine that a moment both players describe as crucial influenced the course of the match, and quite possibly the outcome. Speak to anyone else about which colour haunts Davis most in that contest and they will say the last black in the 35th and deciding frame. But the man himself has always looked at a shot he played on a green when attempting to clear up and make it 9-0. Incredibly, having stolen that frame to get on the board at 8-1, Taylor used it as a springboard to get himself right back in the game, winning seven of eight frames to trail only 9-7 overnight.

Davis says: "I made a flying start, 7-0 in the first session, and then 8-0 after the first of the evening. I had him in an awful situation.

"It is all going to plan, and I really have never understood how I then collapsed other than I must have just, like a long-distance runner, waited for my opponent to catch up.

"There was this moment at 8-0 when I had a decision about whether to take on a green or play safe. It wasn't that poor a decision to take it on. But Dennis was in such a bad place maybe I could have made it worse for him at that moment by tying him up and piling on more pressure.

"Maybe I didn't have to take that chance, and asked him to come up with a tough pot rather than leave it easy. Judging the right shot at the right time was something I was good at, but that is one I would like to have back, play the safety and see what happened. Because I strongly suspect at 9-0, I win that final.

"But I end up going back to the hotel at only 9-7 up, and I am like a bear with a sore head. I couldn't have been in a worse situation being in front, and found it hard to sleep that night, to banish those thoughts. It felt like I was losing.

"We were in for a long day on the Sunday but I was fit and healthy, and adrenaline gets you through. The average frame times were longer then, and the miss rule had a lot to do with that, it wasn't applied like it is today, and that made it easy to survive tactical exchanges."

Taylor says: "And even at 7-0 down after the first session I still hadn't given up hope. I was a bit down, but I was chatting away to fans in the audience in between frames – and speaking to my mum as well to relax.

"In the evening I won a few of the frames in one visit, and that left me feeling a lot better. I understand Steve didn't sleep well that night, but neither did I due to the excitement.

"Steve was probably on a downer, and I was on an upper! I remember my good friend Trevor East of ITV and myself had a bottle of champagne that night.

"That wasn't the usual thing to do and might seem very inappropriate, but I just needed to unwind somehow.

"Steve was all about the choice of shot, and the green in frame nine annoyed him more than the black in the decider, which he had to go for – there was no choice. But that one shot was huge. He normally would have knocked it in, but he could have played safe and put me under even more pressure.

"If that goes in it is 9-0 and the whole match changes. It was a huge turning point in the match, as you so often get in snooker.

"It gave me a first frame, one on the board. Everyone remembers me wagging my finger at the end, but I also did it after that frame – one frame won.

"And then that prompted the comeback in the evening. The breaks started coming and in the end I think it was 13 breaks of over 50 and a couple of high 40s."

Taylor, of course, never led in the match until the end – and so while he drew level on a number of occasions the second day, much as the first, was an exercise in trying to get back on terms and prevent Davis from getting too far ahead.

He adds: "It was a battle. I got back to 11-11, then it was 13-11 behind again ahead of the evening. But given what had happened earlier in the match it just didn't seem to matter any more. He didn't feel safe a couple of frames ahead, and I didn't feel out of it.

"He got out to 15-12, a good lead, but I still thought I could win. I had a lot of things motivating me in that match, it wasn't just the memory of my mum. One of them was a rowdy group of Steve's supporters from Romford.

"They were sitting up in the players' balconies, and if I missed one it was 'Come on Steve, come on my son' and it started to annoy me and wind me up. Things like that can spur you on. A couple of years later at the Masters there was something similar when Howard Kruger bought Alex Higgins a dozen bottles of champagne to celebrate his first big title for a while. But the match wasn't over, I was 8-5 down when I heard what had happened and it drove me on to get the last four frames and win.

"Anyway, that helped me back to 15-15 but he kicked on again to go two up with three to play. At 17-15 some had started to give up on me but I had not given up on myself.

"There were people down at the back of the commentary box I heard afterwards with the big cheque with Steve's name on it – I wonder what that's worth now!"

The two players had given their all, but there was still one, fabled, drama-packed 68-minute final frame to come. It was in truth a horrible frame, reds on cushions everywhere and lengthy safety exchanges, one that might have seen those millions switching off in droves had there not been so much riding on it – but paradoxically that merely ended up further heightening the tension in a match where there had not been a century break.

After 45 minutes of a frame notable for misses, in-offs, and running out of position Taylor led 44-28 but by the time Davis potted the final green he led 62-44, an advantage of 18 with the four colours worth a total of 22 still remaining.

He was also to miss a match-ball brown even before the gut-wrenching denouement.

And the mind-blowing exchange on the last black saw Taylor's attempted double go safe off the knuckle of the middle pocket, the same player miss an attempted pot to the green pocket by a distance, serving up Davis with the cut-back chance that is now the stuff of legend. He over-cut it, putting his hand to an ashen-faced brow – offering Taylor his chance of sporting immortality.

Taylor's recollections of the frame are, as you might expect, vivid. He says: "Anyone watching was sucked in by the drama, and just as well because it did go scrappy.

"There were a lot of reds on cushions, but I would always claim there were some high-quality safety shots from both of us. Listen, at that stage both of our heads were in jam jars and he was getting whiter as I was getting redder.

"Anything could have gone wrong under that pressure, it is about the most intense pressure that any two players can have been under, you had no idea how you would cope, and it was an autopilot job.

"I had a little word with the lady on the top of the trophy after potting the pink, I think it was a case of 'Hopefully I'll be seeing you in a minute if this double on the black goes in.'

"So I walk round to take on the back double – and I thought it was in as the crowd started cheering, but it caught the jaw and very luckily it went safe.

"Steve played a fantastic safety shot from there, I went for a big long double. It was a shot I used to play, and I wasn't going down on a bad safety shot after all the hard work, I was going to have a go.

"Then Steve left me a long black to the green pocket, my first proper chance. I was saying to myself keep the head still, four or five feathers, push the cue out in a straight line.

"But everything moved, my arm went out to the right, one of the biggest twitches at the Crucible. It didn't even get in the jaws. I walked away without looking and thought, 'I've blown it.'

"Only when I turned round it wasn't quite the gimme I thought. Steve said after his limbs didn't feel like his. You would try not to hit that cut thick, but he over-compensated and hit it much too thin.

"And somehow the white made it all around the table, I was so grateful not to have use the rest. I could get my hand on the table, and thankfully this black was easier.

"When it went in the first thing I did was stand there brandishing the cue above my head, then it was stamping it on the floor – and that was 13 years of trying and hope coming out, having been so close in 1979.

"I certainly didn't have any celebration planned, then there was the wagging of the finger to Trevor East saying, 'I told you so!'"

From Davis's perspective, it was a grim end to a day that been spent in a state of shock, and another shot to rue in addition to the decisive black.

He says: "We could hardly pot a ball in that last frame both of us, we were like gibbering wrecks. I missed a pink when I was amongst the balls and I was laughing watching it back on video.

"The whole second day was a blur for me, I just about remember coming to the table to try and pot the last black. But it was surreal, out-of-body stuff. I remember Dennis kissing the trophy, and it was also very exciting to be a part of it. I felt like being on autopilot, it was 100 per cent pressure, and we coped with it as best we could although we were rubbish in that final frame.

"I remember potting the last red into the yellow pocket with the rest, coming off side and top cushions and hanging on to the rest as John Williams was trying to take it back as I willed the white to bounce more off the cushion. Another ball's roll and I could have seen the pink and that might have been the winning shot.

"I don't think I would have missed a straight one on the last black, but I didn't get that. The drama in snooker does come from misses, and there were a lot of mistakes in that final frame. And people were more patient back then, they put up with a 68-minute frame. It is more fast-food today, I think more people might have said it was boring!"

Taylor's finger-wagging towards East, brandishing and then stamping of the cue and kissing the trophy before the presentation are all images burned into the memory.

A stunned Davis was not ready for a microphone when the BBC's David Vine stepped in to the arena, and there were two one-word answers and a "It all happened in black and white" to chew on.

Taylor said to Vine: "It's a good job the black was over the pocket. That's definitely the greatest match I have been involved in in my life." The handing over of a £60,000 cheque was almost immaterial, but the presentation of the trophy was a sweet moment for Taylor.

Davis's manager Barry Hearn thought he had seen most things in sport, but this was new and uncharted territory. Looking back, Hearn says: "You can't lose if you're Steve in that match. You are 8-0 up against Dennis Taylor, you cannot lose, absolutely impossible. But the more you think that, the more likely it becomes.

"People say trite things but you do have to experience defeat, and painful defeat, to be a winner, as Steve did in this one, and against Tony Knowles in 1982. Complacency in life, in business, in sport is the biggest killer out there. After the second session it was already 9-7 and I am asking myself as a manager too, how did I allow that to happen, I have more experience than that.

"It was all over at 8-0, shrug your shoulders, another title done, plan the party and I'm thinking what bottles of red wine to order. Schoolboy errors on our part. Steve would never admit to taking his foot off the gas – but he took his foot off the gas, whether consciously or subconsciously.

"And Dennis was a scrapper with bottle. As a player he wasn't good enough to beat Steve over the best of 35 frames at the Crucible, but be believed he could do it. In a street fight, he was dangerous.

"It is a therapy for 30 years job, what happened in that final frame – him and me. I was backstage behind the curtain, I couldn't go in the arena, or watch.

"Then Dennis played a not great double shot on the black to leave Steve that cut-back, which was not the easiest shot. I never saw that black missed, having just asked, 'Tell me he's got it.' It was a total nightmare, I got extremely drunk afterwards."

With the celebrations or drowning of sorrows both on the night and in the days that followed out of the way, all began to realise the legacy that had been created.

When Davis formally retired from competition in 2016 he said in his parting press conference at the Crucible that the miss on the black against Taylor "was both the best and worst moment of my career, it excited people who before just expected me to win".

Now, he says: "At the party after at the Grosvenor I was having a drink, or several, to try and get over it. I remember Barry sort of joke-headbutting his wife Susan saying 'I love you', she said 'Ow!' and then he headbutted me. Then he dared me to do the same to one of the journalists, and I did! Now the guy wants a fight and the others usher him away. The bloke probably had just cause to sue, but we promised him an exclusive and that seemed to do the trick. And he did a good article, to be fair.

"Dennis and I had to do an exhibition in Reading a few days after, that was when it started to dawn about the impact. There was a lot of interest in us playing each other again. It was a bit strange, but we did our job properly."

But the last words belong to Taylor after the most extraordinary of contests.

He recalls: "There was a celebration in the Crucible, then we went back to the hotel and Rileys had another party and we were up to 6am. But when I got home near Blackburn Golf Club up the hill and through an estate, there were cars parked everywhere.

"My daughter had come over and there was a big banner from the balcony of the house saying 'Welcome home, dad'. There was nothing about being world champion, and that was special.

"Then a few days later I had to go to London and the taxi drivers were all stopping in the road and coming up and shaking my hand. They are a tough crowd, and see all sorts!

"It changed my life, no question. Even last year I got a guy in Ireland asking, 'You still doing the weight-lifting with the cue?' This is more than 30 years ago."

Fan's view, John Airey

The thing I remember most is spending an inordinate amount of time in the Crucible foyer trying to get a ticket for the final session. We hadn't got season tickets that year, but had tickets for all sessions except the very last one. I tried most of the week to get a return but nobody handed any back.

After the first eight frames, there were a few available, but like most people I thought this could be a session to spare job and a waste of 40 quid. However, after the Taylor comeback in session two, I spent just about every spare minute queuing for a return.

The old ticket office was right next to a fetid gents' toilet and it wasn't a pleasant few hours. Finally at about 6pm the kindly ticket lady who must have been sick of me pestering her, smiled and said there had been one handed in.

The match itself, certainly when compared to the modern game, wasn't of the highest quality. I was about six rows back behind Dennis's seat and desperate for him to win. I think as a kid sports results matter more and I was in 'the anyone but Davis' camp.

With hindsight it's a shameful position to have held. Davis winning everything paradoxically blinded me to how good he was. Years later I had a few pints with him one late night in the Mercure Hotel and I got to understand his genuine love for the game and what a decent bloke he is. With a time machine, I'd switch allegiances.

Maybe it's just because the final frame is rerun all the time but that's the one that sticks in the memory. The last brown and blue were fantastic shots from Dennis and when they went in, you knew it was going to the black.

In those days there were no TV screens in the auditorium so unless you were in line with a pocket you couldn't instantly tell whether a ball was on line (that's why you see a lot of people nowadays in the front rows looking up to the TVs above the table to see whether balls are going in).

Consequently, when Dennis went for the double on the black I looked straight at the spectators on 'A' row on the yellow side as they would be the first to know if it was in – one guy screamed it was, but he can't have been a player as it was well onto the top knuckle.

After Steve got the double kiss, Dennis was left the black right into my eyeline into the green pocket. I think Dennis, if he were honest, would say he never had the silkiest cue action, but he really snatched at that black, and pulled it a mile off-line.

I saw the black going round the table and knew he'd lost. I remember just looking at my feet for a few seconds. When I looked up I realised the black wasn't an absolute gimme. It's the type of shot if you were just clearing up after having already won the frame you would just knock in easily on instinct, but into a blind pocket under pressure it was missable.

Steve to his credit missed it on the brave 'thin' side which meant he was leaving the black on if he overcut it. On the winning pot I remember watching Dennis's back hand and he really loosened his grip after the previous miss, he was barely holding the cue.

When he potted it, I remember going berserk. There is some horrendous footage, if you know where to look, of a teenage boy with a dodgy haircut bouncing up and down in a bad suit. I still feel honoured I was the last one in, though.

Chapter 7

Joe Johnson v Steve Davis, 1986, final

"My wife said 'Those shoes look nice', and I replied, 'Those bright pink ones, I can't wear those' — but she insisted they would go well with my grey suit, so I gave in"

THE 1986 World Championship needed some storyline to follow what had gone 12 months' previously, and arguably the biggest accolade that could be paid to the tournament is that it delivered a worthy renewal.

To no great surprise the man to beat once more was Steve Davis, driven on by the hurt of the sensational defeat at the hands of Dennis Taylor, and coming off a season that had seen him win the Singapore Masters, the Grand Prix, the UK Championship and the British Open.

And wins over Ray Edmonds (10-4), Doug Mountjoy (13-5), Jimmy White (13-5) and Cliff Thorburn (16-12) saw him back in the final, an occasion in which he had now featured for five of six seasons.

But who would he face this time? The top half of the draw was given an early shake-up when defending champion Taylor was dumped out by Mike Hallett with a 10-6 win, something that would have offered hope to Alex Higgins, Terry Griffiths, Kirk Stevens and Tony Knowles.

But instead it was another and far lesser known player from nearby Bradford, one who had prior to this year not enjoyed a single win at the Crucible, that took full advantage and stormed through.

If Joe Johnson did not rejoice in a stellar profile in the wider sporting world he was by no stretch of the imagination an unknown within the snooker fraternity, having enjoyed a successful amateur career, before turning professional in 1979.

Tough years followed, but in the 1984–85 campaign Johnson reached the semi-final of the Mercantile Credit Classic, and despite a 10-8 first-round World Championship loss to Bill Werbeniuk that was enough to elevate him into the top 16 for the first time for the following season – and finally the chance to play a qualifier in the first round at the Crucible.

The 150-1 title outsider, now 33, had all the shots and personality to burn, singing in the Preston-based band Made In Japan, possessing the front to break with footwear tradition in the often solemn atmosphere of the Crucible, and having left behind pre-snooker jobs with the gas board as a pipe layer, and as a trainee mechanic.

And his challenge gathered momentum, beating Dave Martin (10-3), Hallett (13-6) and then in the kind of match that sends belief levels soaring Terry Griffiths in the quarter-finals, winning the last four frames for a thrilling 13-12 victory. Knowles was the favourite in the semi-finals but he was despatched 16-8 and once again strong favourite Davis would face a little-fancied underdog opponent in the final.

The BBC and press had latched on to his singing at an early stage, visiting him at his home club, the Morley Snooker Centre, to see his band do a gig. And Johnson's wife Terryll left an impression on the tournament in a way she may not have fully imagined, having picked out for him some pink spats to wear with his grey suit in the afternoon session. The shoes attracted publicity by the bucketload.

Johnson had no airs and graces but loved life and knew deep down he could play a bit, a down-to-earth and pragmatic approach that would stand him in very good stead in the biggest match of his career.

He recalls: "I was a good player and a good pro, had done the exhibitions circuit and paid my dues…but I was just so relaxed coming in to the World Championship that year.

"It was my first year in the top 16, and so for the first time I got to play a qualifier rather than a big name in the first round, which was a huge difference back then.

"I had played at the Crucible before without winning a match, now I had a chance against Dave Martin and was confident of beating him and getting into the last 16.

"And if I did that I knew I would play Dennis Taylor or Mike Hallett. Dennis had beaten me 10-1 at the Crucible two years before so I expected to play him, the defending champion. But Mike beat him and I had always done okay against him and it just seemed it was falling for me.

"I had never beaten Terry Griffiths but from 12-9 down I played probably the best four frames of my life to win 13-12, making a couple of centuries.

"And I did seem to pick up a lot of the neutrals' support. I was from Yorkshire not far from Sheffield, which helped with the crowd actually in the arena. I had a lot of supporters in there for my matches.

"Then there was the singing which the BBC latched on to a bit, and my band Made In Japan. And then of course the shoes that seemed to capture the imagination a bit.

"That was my wife's doing. For the first time ever she came to a tournament with me, and we went out between sessions of one of the early matches.

"She said 'Those shoes look nice', and I told her, 'Those bright pink ones? I can't wear those!' But she insisted they would go well with the grey suit, so I gave in.

"You could wear those shoes in the afternoon, then at night time it had to be the dress suit and black shoes. But I don't think anyone had worn anything like that before.

"The band came down to support me for the whole tournament and after I won my first match we did a show at my club, I did a couple of songs and the BBC filmed it and showed it on the coverage.

"I think my favourite was Everlasting Love by The Love Affair, and we made a record of it soon after the World Championship.

"But coming in to the final Steve Davis was like God at the time, he beat people 10-0 sometimes, I remember him beating Mike Hallett 13-1 in the 1980s. Everybody was afraid to play him and that was usually worth a couple of frames start to him.

"And once he was on top of somebody he generally powered on and steamrollered them. Look what he did to John Parrott in that final, 18-3, and Parrott was one of the all-time greats in my opinion."

But despite his clear respect and admiration for Davis, Johnson did have some reason for hope, stemming from an encounter before the pair had turned professional.

He adds: "I had not played him as a pro, only as an amateur where I beat him 10-1 for money. So maybe the fear factor wasn't there, though we played a few times as amateurs.

"I remember Barry Hearn bringing £4,000 up for one of our matches, and he could only get £200 on Davis, no one wanted to back me to beat Davis despite the 10-1, and I beat him again. Barry took me out afterwards and said, 'Thanks – you've saved me £4,000!'"

For his part Davis, who had seen something in Johnson in his amateur days, could not understand why he had not done more damage in the professional ranks.

He recalls: "Joe could have been described before the 1986 World Championship as a hugely talented underachiever.

"I knew him from amateur days, and when I first bumped into him I remember thinking 'Blimey, this bloke is a bit of a player.'

"He had all the shots in the book, and was really naturally gifted as well as being a lovely guy. And you wondered, 'Why hasn't he done better?' Had he been hiding under a rock, what was going on with him? He was a bit older than I was.

"And you were left thinking that maybe the only possible reason was that he hadn't dedicated himself to snooker enough, and had other things he liked and enjoyed doing.

"It was genuinely a bit of a puzzle as to why he hadn't done better at that time. When the floodgates opened and everyone turned professional he did so, but he hadn't been on the Richter scale before that year.

"He hadn't won a match at the Crucible before 1986, but he had a massive win against Terry Griffiths in the quarters, 13-12 winning the last four frames.

"And that kind of win makes people sit up, they think 'How on earth has he done that against Terry?', who was a real force in the game.'

"You sort of assumed, unfairly on both sides as it turned out, that Terry must have cracked rather than it was down to Joe playing well.

"But I had played exhibitions against him and knew exactly how good he was. He was a really good screw-back player, and a good billiards player.

"That may not mean much to people these days, but having that skill meant he knew what the balls were going to do, how they would react. Joe had a good touch in the balls, and wasn't a banger – there was some class there."

And Davis swiftly realised that while he was for the second year in a row a huge favourite to win a fourth world title, that was where the comparisons stopped as he was faced with a completely different challenge.

A relaxed Johnson was going for his shots, getting most of them, admittedly getting some good run of the balls, but looking for all the world as if he was playing for the light money in his club rather than on the sport's ultimate stage.

Johnson edged the first session 4-3, and then held firm as Davis won the next four frames to respond in kind. At the end of the Sunday night, the scores were locked at 8-8. But when the pair emerged on Monday afternoon Johnson kicked on again, embarking on another four-frame winning streak that meant he had won eight of nine.

Though Davis rallied, including a break of 100 in the last frame of the third session, the Nugget still trailed 13-11 going in to the evening finale.

Johnson says: "Unusually I never practised between the matches, never hit a ball on anything other than the match table. I didn't pick my cue up before the final, I knew it would be a long match and I wanted to be fresh.

"Steve made two centuries in going 3-1 up and I remember sitting in that first mid-session interval in the dressing room thinking, 'I really don't want this to be 18-1.'

"It felt like every frame was a bonus at that stage, but I won the next three to be 4-3 up after the first session, and when it was 8-8 after the first day I felt I could win.

"I thought I hadn't played my best, and I was level, whereas I thought Steve had played pretty well. So I thought I had a great chance if I could keep the pressure on and stay with him.

"But instead it was the other way around, I went clear of Steve. I was 12-8 up, and then 13-11 up at the end of the third session. And before the final session I went for a curry with my managers.

"And that seemed to do the trick. I was careful and didn't eat too much, you didn't want to feel bloated for the final session, but it was relaxing and put me in the right mood. I just had my normal lamb curry, but it was great to escape the mayhem at the Crucible."

If Davis was starting to suffer on day two, he was big enough to recognise the show Johnson was putting on, and his remarkable temperament given the circumstances.

He recalls: "It was a totally different match to the Dennis final. Again I was the heavy favourite, but up against someone with a very different style to Dennis.

"Dennis could make it difficult, and there were going to be safety exchanges. But Joe was playing a free and easy style that put me on the back foot.

"He had the natural ability and crucially enjoyed the occasion, he didn't appear to be overawed in any way by the surroundings or what was at stake.

"I felt like I was playing catch-up the whole game. Against Tony Knowles there were times I wanted the ground to swallow me up.

"And against Dennis I was looking over my shoulder, really uncomfortable. But against Joe I was in the right frame of mind – he was just too strong and held me off.

"He totally outplayed me the whole match, and I didn't have anything like the same feelings as 1985. I held my hands up and said 'Well played'.

"I was a lot more philosophical about the disappointment, I respected his ability and how he had played.

"Joe potted one red all the way down the cushion from the top of the table to the green pocket and those get to you. The crowd were loving it, and while I wasn't loving it I knew he was playing brilliantly.

"It wasn't reckless, he was just playing without a care and no pressure. The crowd were hugely on his side, both for being the underdog and also coming from Yorkshire and not far away. But it wasn't too raucous, and respectful. I wasn't playing the crowd that day, just Joe."

With the winning line in sight Johnson might have been expected to suffer at least some nerves and start to stutter. Instead, he just put his foot down harder on the pedal and accelerated all the way to the title.

And the final flourish, when it came in the 30th frame to clinch an 18-12 victory, was marvellous. Starting from 27-22 behind Johnson waltzed around the table, potting long blues for fun with the black out of commission.

The roars from the crowd came as the match-winning red went down, and as the final blue and pink flew in to complete a break of 64 with the world title long since secured Johnson could be seen smiling and shaking his head. It had really happened, a sporting fairytale.

With the Crucible crowd giving Johnson one of its longest ever standing ovations, the player sat in his chair having lit up a calming cigarette – looking around and taking it all in, finally giving a wave to the crowd.

David Vine, the BBC presenter now in the arena, said: "They'll never stop, Joe. Joe Johnson, from Bradford…snooker champion of the world!"

Johnson replied: "It has been terrific. But what a terrific player Steve is, he still doesn't get the recognition he should have. His ability is second to none, and he is the perfect gentleman on and off the table – a great ambassador for snooker.

"I hope we can still be friends! I learned a lot just playing him, how to keep cool. But I went for a few long pots and got away with a bit today. I had all the running."

Davis, the surprise bridesmaid for a second year in succession, managed to get in a reference to the Taylor final to Vine: "We can't go on meeting like this, David. It is the second time talking to you in this situation."

Quick as a flash and referring to Davis's near inability to speak on that occasion, Vine replied: "And that's twice as much as you said last year!"

But Davis was quick to add: "I got absolutely buried in this final so no complaints, and Joe is a worthy champion."

And though clearly disappointed he was far more accepting of defeat than the previous year, Johnson's brilliance being a less bitter pill to swallow than the huge 8-0 lead tossed away against Taylor.

Davis says: "Even though I ended up losing twice, in two big shocks, in successive years it never really dented my confidence or made me wonder if I would win it again.

"I could stay in the moment or had a plan beyond the next tournament, certainly after winning the world title that first time.

"The only time I changed anything was after that 1985 final loss to Dennis, when as a result I decided not to play in the Irish Masters the following year.

"So this year, the 1986 World Championship, I didn't go to Goffs because it finished so close to the Crucible starting. I think it was the only year I did that.

"I'm not sure whether reaching the final justified that decision, but it was how I felt and what I wanted to do.

"And on Joe, let's not forget, he got to the final again the following year, probably the closest anyone has got to ending the Crucible Curse."

For Johnson there were some memorable celebrations to come – and then life experiences on the back of his exploits that he could not have imagined possible in his wildest dreams.

He remembers: "I had said on the BBC after the final that I was going to the post-match party, but that following that I would be going back to the club in Bradford and anyone who wanted to meet up for a pint, I'd see them back there!

"And half of Bradford and Leeds turned up at the club. They wanted to present the trophy to me at the party, and I couldn't have left the Grosvenor until around 12.30am.

"We were driving back, myself, my managers Wally Springett and John Rukin and I said there might be a couple of people left, it was past 1.30am by this point.

"But when we pulled off the motorway and started driving up towards the club there was traffic backed up – ambulances, police cars, fire engines and I could not believe what was going on.

"I couldn't get into the front door of the club, I had to come in via the cellar. It was the Morley Snooker Centre my club, sadly no longer there. They pulled it down.

"Amazingly after the final Princess Diana invited us out, me and my wife, we were in a long line of people and she singled me out to ask about the shoes so they must have made an impression.

"And that was when she asked if my wife and I would like to go to Wimbledon, and which celebrity I would like to meet – and I said Cliff Richard. So we did, that was a big one for me. My wife wanted to sit next to Diana and I wanted to sit next to Cliff, but we were sat next to the wrong people!"

No ordinary Joe, no ordinary year and once more no ordinary story.

Johnson then returned the following year to prove it was no fluke, getting to the final again only for Davis to exact revenge with an 18-14 win. And the man from Bradford remained the closest to ending the Crucible Curse of first-time winners right up to 2017, having won two more frames than Ken Doherty in 1998 against John Higgins.

But it will be for his shot-making, his shoes, his extra-curricular singing, and his sheer *joie de vivre* in the match that defined his career that Johnson will always be remembered, bringing more than the odd smile to the face along the way.

Chapter 8

Stephen Hendry v Jimmy White, 1992, final

"At 14-8 up I was thinking how I would thank my old headmaster for giving me time off school to go down the snooker club, how I had made it work, and how he should be proud of his decision"

B Y the time Scotland's Stephen Hendry and England's Jimmy White met in what was their second World Championship final clash in 1992, the match-up was whetting all possible appetites.

The Whirlwind, already featured in these pages, had only missed the chance of a place in the showpiece in 1982 thanks to being on the wrong end of one of the greatest breaks in the tournament's long history from Alex Higgins in the semi-final.

However, White had bounced back just two years later, making the final at the age of just 22, losing to another long-time rival Steve Davis 18-16. At that time a carefree White barely gave the loss a second thought, so sure was he that further opportunities to win the big one would come along. And so they did in the 1990s.

At that time the popularity of the People's Champion had if anything increased, with the era of Ronnie O'Sullivan yet to start, and 'Hurricane' Higgins' career all but blown out. White had become a byword for flair and panache at the table, and though he did not always win, he rarely disappointed his loyal supporters in the entertainment stakes, carrying as he did a ready-made arena atmosphere around with him.

But White, who turned 30 during this World Championship, was now in his prime as a player. Despite the three Crucible final defeats up to this point, including an unexpected one to an inspired John Parrott the previous year, he had racked up seven ranking titles and was the sport's biggest box office draw.

The bad news for White was that Hendry was also approaching his prime years, and though no one could yet know quite the dominant force the Scot would become the signs were ominous from a player that was to revolutionise the way snooker was played.

Before Hendry arrived on the scene, turning professional in 1985, Scotland's only previous world champion had been Walter Donaldson, with two final victories over Fred Davis in 1947 and 1950. But the boy from South Queensferry quickly set about making his own history.

Hendry may have lost his Crucible debut at 17, famously being applauded out of the arena by Willie Thorne after he finished a relieved 10-8 winner, but a first ranking title was not long in coming, the Grand Prix in 1987.

Hendry became the youngest ever world champion at 21 years and 106 days in 1990, beating White 18-12 in the final, but his impact on the game was about more than the titles he was racking up. Hendry was utterly fearless, grabbing frames and matches by the throat, going for the jugular with an all-or-nothing attacking approach. Invariably this strategy yielded rich dividends and plenty of 'one-visit snooker', allied as it was to a ruthless nature and ice-cool temperament. And his influence on those that followed was profound.

Hendry had unexpectedly lost to Steve James in the quarter-finals in 1991 as he attempted to end the 'Crucible Curse' of first-time defending champions, but in 1992 in Sheffield he had beaten Stephen Murphy, James Wattana, Dene O'Kane and Terry Griffiths with relatively little fuss or bother, giving up just 23 frames in reaching the final, against the 52 he had won.

White was pushed a little harder by Canadians Alain Robidoux in the last 16 (13-11) and Jim Wych in the quarter-finals (13-9), and had also beaten Tony Drago (10-4) and then Alan McManus (16-7) in the semi-finals.

Once again the battle lines were drawn for a final between at that time the two best players, and the two best Crucible performers, in the world. And world No.1 Hendry, as ever, was supremely confident.

He says: "Sometimes it was viewed as a clash of styles with me and Jimmy, but we were both fundamentally very attacking players in our own way. Though you could certainly say there was a clash of personalities, in the sense we were just so different.

"By the time of the 1992 World Championship we were both starting to reserve our best snooker for the Crucible. So a rivalry was growing, but even though this sounds strange when you consider how tough so many of our matches were, I always felt comfortable playing Jimmy.

"I always felt the way he played, it was a good match-up for me, that I would get chances – as opposed to someone earlier in my career like Steve Davis, where it could be a tougher match, with 10–15 minute safety exchanges and a different type of game.

"I always felt there were misses in Jimmy as well as the brilliance he was capable of, and that could tell over the longer matches at the Crucible. Of course that doesn't guarantee anything, he beat me at the Crucible a couple of times – but I was never as apprehensive playing him as Steve earlier on, and then a John Higgins or a Ronnie later on. Basically I just thought I had the beating of him if I played to my best level."

White, the world No.3, had enjoyed a good second half of the season, winning the European Open and British Open titles, and finishing runner-up to John Parrott in the UK Championship. And in the first round against Drago he had made only the second 147 maximum break seen at the Crucible, and the first of his career.

White says: "At that time I was basically playing the best snooker of my career. I was highly ranked, was winning titles and regularly getting to finals and the latter stages, and beating the other top players at various times.

"The way the ranking system worked then it was very important to beat the players you should have beaten in the early rounds, and I was doing that.

"But Hendry at that time was also getting stronger and stronger, having won his first world title in 1990 and starting to dominate. I think in that 1991–92 season, even not counting the World Championship, he won something like seven other titles so you could see what he was doing.

"His mindset and temperament and concentration at that time was I believe the best there has ever been in snooker. Mine was never on that level, because my sort of lifestyle was all over the place, though I tried to at the same time be dedicated to my sport."

The Londoner was once again the fans' choice to win the match and secure that elusive world title, but Hendry was never one to be fazed by losing a popularity contest.

He recounts: "I could blank it out, the crowd pulling for Jimmy. I knew from my time in snooker that he was the most popular player, and that was normal. You didn't get upset they weren't cheering for you, you just expected it and had to deal with it. You took it for granted, and didn't take it personally. If there were boos, you would use it.

"It was always much worse at the old Wembley Conference Centre than it was at the Crucible against Jimmy anyway. There you had 2,500 Londoners shouting 'Miss' when you were down on the shot, and you wanted to stick it up them. The Crucible audience was fairer, and not as rough."

White displayed good form at the start of the match, and after watching Hendry knock in a break of 105 for starters responded with breaks of his own of 70, 100 and 68 in taking a 4-3 lead at the end of the first session.

And he kept the pedal down in the second, evening session on the Sunday, extending his advantage to 10-6 overnight. Just eight more frames required, and after taking four of the next six frames on the Monday afternoon, White stood at 14-8 ahead and seemingly on the brink. Even BBC commentator Clive Everton, not given to overstatement or wild predictions, thought the title could finally now be heading White's way. Hendry took the next, but the final frame of the session was to prove pivotal, and it was a typical death-or-glory clutch pot from the Scot that tilted the match in his favour.

With White leading both 14-9 and 53-1 in frame 24 he missed a straightforward red with the frame and a 15-9 advantage at his mercy. And that allowed Hendry to step in, and clear with a break of 64 that included a characteristically brave and brilliant pot on the brown off the final red, after the cue ball had come to rest close to the side cushion and over the jaws of the middle pocket.

Hendry recalls: "I know people were starting to give it to Jimmy at 12-6 up, and then 14-8 of course. And don't get me wrong, I am not feeling good out there at 14-8 down in the final. Six frames behind is not a good situation, and whatever your self-belief if you are not at the table, you can't do anything.

"If they are playing better than you on the day, that's snooker and you can't get at the table. I haven't watched it back a lot but I do remember in the third session he started to get a wee bit edgy, and that opened the door a little. I won the last two of the third session, and that opened the door.

"There are certain shots that you remember in your career, and the brown at 14-9 to help me get back to 14-10 is certainly one of those. There was a blue with a rest against Davis in the UK final, and that brown…the easy shot was to roll up to the black and snooker him.

"But that is not the way I ever played, I saw the shot and didn't hesitate, didn't even think about playing the safety. And if I miss it, I am six behind at 15-9 and he probably wins. It was a big shot, and I honestly believe that shot won me the World Championship, as going in to the night session I then fancied it so, so much even at 14-10."

White admits that he had been planning his acceptance speech with the lead at 14-8. And he, too, acknowledges how important that 24th frame was in the final analysis, given his inability to alter the course of the contest and halt the inexorable Hendry charge.

He says: "In that 1992 final, people always say I cracked up at the end and that is why I lost it, which is basically true. But I look further back in the match as well, I was all over him for a lot of that final and really I could have been further clear.

"There was one frame when I was 50-odd ahead and missed a red when I could have played a different shot, I think it was at 14-9. And that was the difference between being 15-9 going in to the evening, and 14-10 which it ended up being.

"At 14-8 I was sitting there in my chair thinking how I was going to thank my old headmaster for giving me time off school to go down the snooker club and practise, and how I had made it work and he should be proud and pleased with his decision.

"I was thinking I will thank this person, not thank that person, and it didn't really matter to me at that moment whether he won the last two frames of the session or not, I was going to win.

"Then all of a sudden he started to get a lot stronger, and because I had lost my focus I couldn't live with him in that spell of the match. By the end I couldn't have won if he had put the balls over the holes, I was gone. I had lost all focus and sense of where I was and the match situation.

"It is a horrible feeling when it happens to you out there, but when it all starts going wrong the self-doubt creeps in and you start to question everything. You question your cue action, the pockets look smaller, the other guy gets a lift from seeing what is happening to you.

"And it is one of the reasons I am such a fan of Mark Selby now. He comes from a snooker hall and pool hall background, and he is not bothered about anything, and is just pleased to be there. In that area of mental strength, he is very similar to Hendry."

If there were two key frames in the final from Hendry's perspective, the second of them was the opener in the final, evening session with the score at 14-10 to White.

Frame 25 was a scrappy affair, with both players having chances to take it. White led 61-30 with one red left, but twitched at it while arguably over-stretching – allowing Hendry, now utterly convinced he would win the match, to clear with 33 to win it on the black.

Hendry says: "I have come out at 14-10 down and the first frame was really scrappy, it could have gone either way. And having just managed to win it I just remember looking over at Jimmy and you could sense when he was under pressure. He would towel his face, run his hands through his hair, hit balls too hard, sweat more...I could tell when he was under it.

"But it was after that first frame of the night that I thought I had him, and that was massive. We both had loads of chances, and Jimmy twitched on a red late on in the frame and after that I pretty much ran away with it, finishing with a 50-odd and then two centuries.

"I had all the momentum and was just in my groove, and by that stage not looking at him any more. I was doing my own thing, and going through those last frames. And when I was in the zone I could frighten other players, focused, just me on the table and I never missed."

Hendry finished up by astonishingly taking the last ten frames in a row, an 18-14 winner after trailing White 14-8. It was a cruel and bitter blow for the left-hander, who had lost two key frames in a row at a time when he may not have fully recognised their importance.

Once again, White had not come up with what he needed in a Crucible final, his fourth, to get the job done. He had scored just 80 points in the last six frames, Hendry making breaks of 134 and 112 with the winning line beckoning to secure victory and a second world title. It was, White admits, the worst, most crushing loss of his life given what was at stake, and the match situation.

He adds: "Hendry in that match had all but accepted that he was not going to win, because I was outplaying him in every department of the game. But because he is such a prolific winner and had such self-belief he knew that there was a chink and when I wilted, he could get stronger. That is what he held on to even when it might have seemed hopeless, and when the opportunity came he took it.

"It was like he went at the flick of a switch from playing at 60 per cent, to playing at 100 per cent, and I couldn't stop him because I had lost my focus. And that has to be the most disappointing loss of my life, for sure, given where I was and how I had been playing."

For Hendry though, the win and the manner of it merely confirmed what he already believed – that was the man to beat, the undisputed No.1 player, and that this was still only the beginning.

Andy Roddick was once asked about his lop-sided rivalry with Roger Federer in tennis, after losing yet another high-profile match to him in one of the four Majors. In all Roddick won three of 24 matches against Federer, and none out of eight in the four Slam events including four finals.

In response to the question, Roddick replied: "I'm gonna have to start winning some of the matches to call it a rivalry."

White had a far better record against Hendry than Roddick against Federer, and could point to wins in a ranking event final and twice at the Crucible. Nevertheless, this was the direction in which the Hendry/White clashes were heading unless the Whirlwind could do something about it in the years to come.

Hendry adds: "Jimmy beat me in plenty of tournaments, and also at the Crucible a couple of times. It was a great rivalry in the sense we played several huge finals in quick succession at the Crucible, and it was the match everyone wanted to see. Maybe Jimmy would have had to win at least one of those finals for it to be a truer sporting rivalry.

"But we did play each other in all those Crucible finals, and then there was the nature of those encounters themselves, they made for compelling viewing. We did joke in the practice room at one point, 'The other 30 players shouldn't bother turning up, it is us again!'

"It was very satisfying personally to come from that far down in this one and win the title with ten frames in a row. It makes you feel invincible, that you deserve to be world champion and world No.1."

Chapter 9

Stephen Hendry v Jimmy White, 1994, final

"He's beginning to annoy me"

W HEN Jimmy White made it through to a sixth World Championship final in 1994, a fourth against Stephen Hendry and a third in a row against the Scot who remained the world No.1 and strong title favourite at the Crucible, there was an inevitable sense of 'it's déjà vu all over again'.

The Whirlwind was only 31 years of age as the sport's elite headed for the Crucible that spring, not old either in comparison to those that had gone before and won the title, or since.

White had played the season ranked No.3 once again, and although it had not been the most startling campaign there had been semi-final appearances at the European Open, International Open and Thailand Masters.

But the Crucible was where White had played some of the best snooker of his career, and there was at least little doubt he would once again step up to the plate. The real questions were whether that would be good enough to topple Hendry, now such a fearsome and dominant force, and if it was possible for any sportsperson to overcome the mental scars of what had gone before in this particular match-up in this tournament.

White began his 1994 event with a routine 10-6 win over Scotland's Billy Snaddon before being given a sterner test by Neal Foulds, eventually prevailing 13-10. After being locked at 8-8 White won five of the next seven frames to get over the winning line, suggesting his nerve remained intact.

White had always been a brave player, and he withstood another attempted comeback from Ken Doherty in the quarter-finals, after the Irishman had closed from 12-7 to 12-10 before the match was closed out with a break of 83.

And with a growing sense of inevitability about who might once again feature in the showpiece, Darren Morgan could do nothing to stop that, White winning 16-8 in the semi-finals.

Hendry, for his part, was now a three-time world champion and supremely confident of adding another title to his CV. Following the 1992 Crucible final he had crushed White 18-5 the following year, a marker that suggested the Londoner simply could not beat him over the best of 35 frames.

During the season, Hendry had won the European Open and the Dubai Classic, but lost in the final of the UK Championship to teenage sensation Ronnie O'Sullivan, an emerging threat to his hegemony, and in the final of the Masters to compatriot Alan McManus.

Once in Sheffield he gave up just three frames in reaching the quarter-finals with wins over Surinder Gill (10-1) and Dave Harold (13-2). Nigel Bond did better, but went down 13-8, and with another White showdown looming there was a comfortable 16-9 victory over Steve Davis, whose powers were fading and left him largely unable to match Hendry at this stage of an illustrious career.

So the stage was set once again, the clash everyone wanted to see, but one popular outcome most hoped for, and quite another pragmatic one that the vast majority expected. After the previous two years, seeing White snatch defeat from the jaws of victory in the 1992 final and then being crushed in 1993, the idea of seeing the People's Champion beat Hendry at this stage of the tournament was looking like wild hope over evidence-based analysis.

And yet White's quest to finally end his agony and secure a first world title had captured the imagination of millions, including those well outside the usual snooker bubble. It had become a sporting parable about dealing with adversity, shaking yourself down and coming back for more, whatever the personal pain and anguish. Only a player whose love for the sport shone brighter than most could have put himself through it.

And the cliché so often heard from long-suffering football fans, 'It's the hope that kills you', was never used in a more appropriate setting than for White and his many supporters over the pursuit of his own Holy Grail.

Whatever pain he had dished out to White, Hendry retained a huge respect for his opponent.

It was White he had idolised when first taking up the game at the age of 12, although Steve Davis usurped the Whirlwind as Hendry's role model during the 1980s. The Nugget was the winning machine that Hendry himself aspired to be.

He recalls: "When I first got a table at home for Christmas and started watching on TV, well before I started on tour and turned pro, Jimmy was my hero. You had Steve Davis, Alex Higgins, Ray Reardon out there but I loved Jimmy's cue action and his style of play, the shots he played.

"I had gone to see him at an exhibition with my dad in Scotland and I used to love watching him. I remember playing him very early in my career in Scotland, I just sat in my chair in awe of him as he beat me 5-0 or 5-1 or something.

"My manager at the time Ian Doyle gave me a kick up the backside and said, 'You're not going to go far if you sit there admiring these people.'

"But as my career progressed and I looked at what I wanted to do in the game, I started to look more to Steve Davis as my example because he was the best, and he was winning all the time, not just the odd tournament like Jimmy. And winning all the time was what I wanted to do, so I stopped idolising Jimmy so much.

"The only way I would have allowed sentiment in and wanted for Jimmy to win one was if he was playing someone else in the final. I got on well with him and respected him as a player and as a bloke. He took defeat incredibly well given how much some of them must have hurt.

"These big finals where he lost them from well ahead or in the final frame, at the party afterwards you would never have known outwardly though he must have been devastated inside. I would never have been able to do that, I couldn't do it.

"You wouldn't want to change him for the world, he is a great guy. But we have all heard sportsmen or pundits or sports psychologists saying, 'Show me a good loser, and I'll show you a loser.' Is there any truth in that? Maybe you do have to have a nasty streak to win what you should."

White acknowledged the hurt felt from his three world final losses to Hendry prior to 1994, and by now five in total, but the flame of self-belief, almost miraculously, still burned within him even if not quite so brightly as before.

"I had obviously taken some bad and hurtful beatings from Stephen in the finals of 1990, 1992 and then again in 1993, which wasn't even close. And maybe it surprised some people that here I was again, back in the final, refusing to go under or go away.

"But for all the pain I was still in there fighting and still believed I could win a world title. And the basic reason for that if I am honest, is that deep down I still thought I was the better player when I was at 100 per cent.

"In my 40s and 50s me winning the World Championship has been pretty much impossible, but back then I was one of the best players in the world, and when I was on my game there weren't many that could live with me.

"And without that belief, there would have been no point playing in these events. I always thought, right from 1984 when I first got in the final, 'I'll just win it the year after, or the year after that.' Then you lose in four more finals in a row, and the scars are building up.

"But as I say, I still thought, rightly or wrongly, that I was the better player if I was playing to the best of my ability and I honestly don't think I would have kept getting to the final had I not believed that."

It was, though, far easier for Hendry to approach the final with confidence. Not only was he by some distance the best player in the world, he had developed the winner's aura that was so often worth frames before a match had even started.

And though it would be quite wrong to say the pressure was off Hendry, since the expectations he had were huge and essentially involved going home with the trophy, the fact is that he had already won three times at the Crucible, and he also knew just how much it hurt White that his name was not yet carved on the silverware.

Hendry says: "Every time I drove down to Sheffield from Scotland in the 1990s to the Crucible, I expected to win the tournament. I remember saying to Mandy once, 'Pack that jacket, I will wear that to the final.' It was matter of fact, but that is how I thought. I literally thought I would win every time.

"And it felt like I owned the place, and the arena. But I didn't say those things in public, it was inward, for me alone. You start saying that and you set yourself up for a fall. And inwardly I almost took it for granted that I would win, I was so confident there.

"I can't put myself in Jimmy's head and speak for him, but you have to imagine that was a factor, that he had lost the last four finals in a row, and three of them to the same person – me. And now he was playing me again.

"To be fair to him one of Jimmy's attributes was that he could leave past results in the past, this was a new match. If it had been me, I would have been the last opponent I would have wanted to face again.

"But despite all the baggage I can't say I was surprised that he took it all the way in this final – the bottom line is that he was a great snooker player. People forget how good he was, perhaps because in recent years they have seen a lesser imitation of the player he was. But he was a great player.

"He was beating everyone else in the game, it just so happened his game suited me. And to get to the final again showed how good he was."

The final, as in 1985 for Steve Davis and Dennis Taylor, and later in 2002 between Hendry and Peter Ebdon, was to come down to a decider, plenty more of which later. But well before that there was a factor in play that had unsettled White, and seemed to have eased any pressure on Hendry.

After the straightforward win over Harold in the last 16, Hendry and his camp revealed that he had slipped in his hotel room overnight between sessions and fractured the elbow of his left, bridging arm. Hendry was quick to refute any allegations floating around at the time of kidology, but White was later to admit that the knowledge of the incident had got into his head and affected him. It seems highly unlikely it made much material difference to the outcome, given how well White played and competed, but was something both players recall vividly.

White admits: "We had the story in the papers about Hendry breaking his arm in his hotel room or whatever, and I think that did actually affect me a bit more than it should have.

"Once again I was all over him in the second session, but the injury thing did play on my mind – maybe it was meant to! I should have been able to dismiss it, but it got to me for whatever silly reason. And I tried to force the issue and win it early doors to kill him off, but I never managed to do it."

Hendry, though, insists: "That was the year when I fractured my elbow. I was 7-1 up on Dave Harold after the first evening session in the second round, and I got up in the night to go to the toilet with no light on. And I slipped on the carpet and broke my elbow.

"I woke up unable to straighten my left arm and had to go to the hospital early the next morning, and you could see an inch fracture the Friday before the afternoon second session. I thought my World Championship was over, the pain was getting down and coming up, once on the table I was fine. The referee was having to get the rest for me, because I couldn't. And it wasn't one we could keep quiet, there were press pictures the next day with me wearing a sling. Ian, to be fair, thought it wasn't a bad idea to tell everyone once it had happened. I know some people wondered if he was engineering some kidology, but I was really hurt – I couldn't play golf all summer either! Had I not been involved in the World Championship, they would have plastered it up properly."

Hendry got off to a good start, leading 5-2 after the first session – but White managed to win seven of the next nine frames to lead 9-7 at the end of the first day's play. Was this really, finally, on? To no one's great surprise the Scot levelled at 12-12 after the third session, setting up a gripping and thrilling climax on the evening of Monday, 2 May – also White's 32nd birthday.

He adds: "Hendry was the hardest player in the world to beat at that time, and unfortunately my game was made for him in the sense that he was such a good potter and I attacked the game too, he took all the chances that I kept serving up. Someone like Selby of the modern era would have slowed him down and stopped him potting all those mad balls. But because my game was attacking, I was tailor-made for him and he was able to pick me off."

But in this final, unlike the previous three between the pair, Hendry had not simply been able to pick White off and the Whirlwind stayed with him. Though he trailed 15-13 and 16-14, White managed to level at 16-16 helped by a supreme example of sportsmanship. White was snookered and failed to get out of it, prompting the referee to call a free ball.

The score was 66-34 and Hendry's lead in the frame therefore 32 points with one red left, but after looking hard at the decision the Scot asked the official to check it once again, and the decision was reversed. Hendry then lost the frame.

White was then to level once again at 17-17, forcing a never-to-be-forgotten deciding frame.

Hendry says: "I was a couple of frames clear twice late on, and that stage of a final it is a bit like a Rocky movie, he gets a punch in, you get one back, frame for frame. That is how it feels. You want the chance to win, and I didn't have a good one at 17-16, he made a good 75 to level it up at 17-17 and we were going all the way."

Though in 1992 White had been close to the title in the sense he led 14-8 and was well clear, he still on that occasion needed four more frames. This year, he was to fall short by just a few balls because in 1994 the final really was all about frame 35.

Hendry was in first in the decider but took on and missed a very tough red, breaking down on 24. White had some work to do but having accomplished much of it, helped by a great pot on a red with the long rest, was on a break of 29 – in the balls, and on the black.

He had a lead of 37-24, and the frame, match and at last the world title seemed to be at his mercy as he settled to take on a black sitting invitingly on its spot. But whether it was a twitch or just a rank poor shot White rushed it. The black, never looking like going in, hit the near jaw, and Hendry was out of his chair like a greyhound. It was a horrible moment for White, one that brought gasps from the audience, and had millions of White fans watching on TV hurling objects at the set.

And if there was one certainty, it was that Hendry would not pass up the opportunity proffered. Despite wobbling one pink in the jaws with the rest he cleared up with a break of 58 to seal a fourth world title, and leave White reeling, the dream ended for another year – and quite possibly forever.

It is clearly a final, and a moment, that Hendry will never forget. He says: "The atmosphere in that last frame was fantastic, and I do think that even the partisan element wavers a little in a match like that because the crowd appreciate what they are seeing. They are so involved, and the oohs and aahs are for both players, even if most still wanted Jimmy to win.

"And with Jimmy on a break and in the balls I am not expecting him to miss. You hope, but I thought it was gone. I gave a friend of mine in the balcony a little look as if to say, 'I'm not coming back to the table here, maybe this is it.' And then from nowhere, a couple of shots later, he twitched the black off the spot.

"I don't think I have ever got out of my chair as fast as that. He had done a lot of the hard work in that break, and was now in good position. In the back of your mind you hope he can miss, but the pessimist in me was winning at that time.

"In terms of a shot a player would never forget, possibly the only worse one was Steve Davis missing that black against Dennis. For Jimmy that black...I mean I look back at the black I missed against Williams in the Masters final, that hurt, but this was on a different scale.

"I know I would have been absolutely devastated. Put it this way, it wouldn't have been much of an interview with David Vine after. He made a quip about me, and even that he said with a rueful smile.

"A black on the spot and the reds at your mercy to finally win your first world title, and fulfil your dream, it must have been horrendous. And he came out and did the interviews with David Vine, you could tell he was gutted but he did it. And at the party he didn't look like that had just happened to him.

'My sponsors had told me they would buy me a Bentley if I won the World Championship and you shouldn't be thinking about that, and I hadn't been until I got to the yellow. And then it suddenly flashed through my mind, 'I could be getting a Bentley here as well.' It was a Continental, a £200,000 Bentley, almost as much as the first prize. I think I only drove it twice, ridiculous really.

"I have felt a bit like the man that killed Bambi's mum at times, you get reminded that often. If I get asked ten questions from fans, six of them will be 'Why didn't you let Jimmy win one?' He was so popular. But it is sport, and we are there to win.

"The same two players in the final three years in a row, four times in five years...it was something. He was in five finals in a row, which when you think about it in today's terms is incredible. But to do that, six in total, and not win one of them there had to be something missing that you need to win."

Forced into the obligatory post-match arena interview with David Vine on the BBC, White managed a rueful: "He's beginning to annoy me...but I'll be back next year."

And of course, the shot that White would most like to have back from his entire career is the one he still gets asked most about. Life in the public eye can indeed be cruel.

He says: "I was really trying to stay in the moment in that break in the decider, and not get ahead of myself. But that is exactly what I did. I rushed that black, I am looking two or three shots ahead, and when I have watched it back it just looks like I think I have won it.

"The black at the end, I just hit it quick, my arm doesn't go through straight. I just got down to it and thought I just have to pot this and I am on the red, and I didn't give the shot enough care or respect and consideration. It was a massive twitch, like you can get in golf with the yips when putting.

"It is amazing though, I still have to console other people now almost on a daily basis and after a while you do realise that there are others out there who were almost more upset and disappointed than you were, incredible as that might sound.

"That is part of it, and part of it comes from there being fewer TV channels in the 1980s especially so there was a large and loyal following for us. But I am very proud of the support I have got and have always had, and continue to have.

"But listen, no one should feel sorry for me, I have had a hoot at this and I still am. As we are having this conversation I am on a friend's yacht in Marbella – just chilling! There isn't much I would change, not at all."

Fan's view: John Airey

The Long Bar in the Crucible in the mid-1980s was a slightly seedier but a much more interesting place than it is today. Those were the days of gambling tax, so unlicensed bookies with suitcases of cash would offer better odds than the official Ladbrokes booth to plenty of willing punters.

People like 'Little Nick', 'The Tweed' and 'Gold Tooth Dave'. As a teenager I spent many hours there after watching every frame in the theatre. About 1984 or 1985 I met a lovely old guy reading the *Racing Post* who I just initially knew as Tommy.

He liked whisky and the horses and started asking me to put his reverse forecasts and accumulators on. It was only the next year that I realised his surname was White, and he was Jimmy's dad. Over the next decade I would share his disappointments as his beloved son just kept coming up short.

In 1994 Tommy had got me a players' pass into the balcony boxes overlooking the table. These give you a superb view of the table but aren't exactly luxurious as you end up sitting on pushed together hard wooden chairs. In those days security was a bit laxer, especially where Jimmy was concerned and he seemed to have no problem getting vast numbers of guest passes for his friends and family.

I can remember looking down on the action and thinking one, that Jimmy was getting a bit thin on top and two, wishing he would buy a suit and shirt that he was comfortable with as he always seemed to be fidgeting and adjusting his collar and cuffs.

The final night I was sitting with Tommy but he couldn't bear to watch and kept nipping out to the bar for a scotch and some fresh air. I remember the overall standard was pretty good and the match had been nip and tuck after Stephen had taken an early lead.

The last frame nobody in the box could watch. Stephen got in early and I thought it could be all over but he missed a tricky red and left it over the pocket. A couple of shots later Jimmy went to split the pack and finished on nothing.

They say it's the hope that kills you and when Jimmy cut in a really difficult red with the long rest, I started to think this might be his year. He'd split the reds and after another good positional shot off the next blue he was in prime position.

I can't honestly say I saw a twitch on the next black. Jimmy's always had a fast cue action with a fast transition at the back, and to me it just looked like a rushed bad miss. Anyway, miss it he did and by a long way.

Looking back now I think the highest accolade I could give Stephen was that I thought he was a certainty to clear up from behind in a world final decider. His nerve under pressure was the best I've ever seen.

The saddest bit for me came later. I went out to the bar and had a drink with Tommy, his friends and my mum and dad. They all left after a while to go to the organised final party with the Embassy people. I hung around a little longer to let the place quieten down and had one more drink on my own.

When I left I was walking down the main staircase out into the foyer and coming the other way was one of Jimmy's young daughters in tears. I wasn't sure what to do so just smiled at her as we crossed trying to offer her some understanding. She stopped and turned round and said, 'Are you laughing at me?' which I certainly wasn't, but thought that was a very brave thing for a young girl to do. I felt like crying myself then.

Chapter Ten

Stephen Hendry v Ronnie O'Sullivan, semi-final, 1999

"This one has been absolutely terrific…
snooker from the gods"

BY the time Stephen Hendry and Ronnie O'Sullivan met for the second time at the World Championship, the Scot was channelling his entire and considerable energies into claiming world title number seven while the man becoming known to all as the Rocket was still chasing his first.

Hendry, already featured in these pages, had gone on from his famous final victory over Jimmy White in 1994 to lift the trophy in both of the next two years, making it at that time a staggering six times in seven years before Ken Doherty and John Higgins halted the charge in 1997 and 1998.

He had though slipped down to No.2 in the world rankings for the season after Higgins' debut Crucible success the previous year, and by his own elevated standards arrived in Sheffield decidedly unhappy with his season's efforts – that despite winning the Scottish Open and Irish Masters.

But if Hendry remained the dominant force in the game, and especially at the World Championship and the Crucible, an arena he regarded as a cross between a personal fiefdom and his living room, there were new and exciting challengers.

Fellow Scot Higgins had already served notice of his intent – and O'Sullivan and Wales's Mark Williams, two other young players that turned professional in the same golden summer of 1992, had also been racking up the titles on tour.

But the undoubted box office star of them all, a mantle he has had to carry for some 25 years and counting at the time of writing, was O'Sullivan.

From the moment O'Sullivan burst on to the professional scene the combination of sheer speed of thought and execution at the table, extraordinary shot-making ability, put together with a rebellious streak, a grimly compelling family back-story and ongoing career-long battles with various demons made for an intoxicating mix that proved utterly irresistible.

Swiftly and almost inevitably dubbed 'The Rocket', O'Sullivan was to prove a worthy heir to the 'People's Champion' tag, and elements of both the brilliance and self-destructive capacity of Alex Higgins were there for all to see.

What was beyond question was that like Higgins and Jimmy White before him, O'Sullivan was making more people tune in to watch snooker on TV than anyone else, and getting more kids to go out, buy a cue, and hit the local club table than any rival.

This was to be a third Crucible semi-final in four years for O'Sullivan, having lost to Peter Ebdon in 1996 and John Higgins in 1998, but at the age of 23 he had already won six ranking titles and a Masters.

And that, with the big breakthrough coming at the 1993 UK Championship at the age of 17, against a backdrop of as a 16-year-old seeing father Ronnie Sr sent to prison for murder.

And he had made other impressions in the famous auditorium, not least for the fastest 147 maximum break in history in 1997, in just five minutes and 20 seconds, against Mick Price.

So this semi-final clash brought together the dominant force, and the man who would be king – something had to give, and an audience expecting a classic in the four-session encounter were not to be disappointed.

O'Sullivan knew exactly what he was up against. He had beaten Hendry already in big matches, including twice in UK Championship finals – but this was the Crucible and the World Championship, against the man who had already won it on half a dozen occasions.

O'Sullivan, who came past Leo Fernandez (10-3), Joe Perry (13-8) and John Parrott (13-9) to reach the semi-final, says: "I loved to watch Stephen Hendry in the 1990s, including the Jimmy finals. But all of his matches were great to me because I just enjoyed watching him beat people up, and score so heavily.

"Sometimes you would be on the next table and all you could hear was break after break after break. You just knew hearing the click of the balls and the scores being announced the other side of the curtain that Hendry was on it again this year.

"It was his back yard, and it was easy to feel like an afterthought at the beginning. That comes from winning five times on the trot."

"I was not by that time confident that I could beat Stephen over the best of 33 frames in what everyone saw as his back yard at the Crucible.

"I had beaten him and had my successes in the sport already, but I hadn't won a world title and Stephen was going for a seventh World Championship win. I knew there was an opportunity and a possibility to win, and that I might beat him, but it wasn't real confidence."

While Hendry always headed south for Sheffield expecting to win, he had missed out on the silverware for the previous two seasons and also had a healthy respect for his talented opponent, regarding him as a genuine world title contender.

He says: "Ronnie might not have won a world title at that time, but he was already one of the best players in the world and someone you would regard as a danger and a threat to you winning tournaments.

"John Higgins, Ronnie and Mark Williams were the three that came through together, and from the mid to late 1990s they were the three to look out for from my perspective.

"I did feel that I was the best player at that time and ahead of the rest, and especially at the Crucible over distance – but that on any given day you could lose to any of them, because they were just very good players.

"Maybe I was a little surprised that Ronnie had not already won a world title by that time. He had won big tournaments and you expected him to win it at some stage. But on the other hand it takes some winning at the Crucible and I still believed that I was the man to beat.

"I just generally didn't look at other players and think about their situation, I just looked at myself and what I was doing.

"I had a tough draw on paper that year, because I had Paul Hunter in the first round and beat him 10-8. Then it was James Wattana in the last 16, that was 13-7, and I did not expect to beat Matthew Stevens by as big a margin as 13-5 in the quarters, but I played well in that match.

"I still didn't see other players as obstacles because if I played well I backed myself to win. And Ronnie wasn't yet the factor in Sheffield that he was, say, by 2002, when I really saw a semi-final against him as the final before playing Ebdon. This one felt like what it was, a semi-final.

"The seventh world title and getting the record was on my mind that year, of course it was. I had actually had a poor season by my standards.

"I lost 9-0 to Marcus Campbell at the UK, and lost three times to Tony Drago in the same season, having never lost to him in my whole career. So these things were on my mind.

"A couple of months before the World Championships I went back to basics and pounded the hours on my own, so I wasn't in the most confident place a couple of months before the event, but that was starting to change as I moved through the draw."

It was no accident that so often in high-profile matches Hendry would emerge from the traps like a greyhound. It was something he worked on, and part of a psychological plan to weaken the resistance of any opponent, and reinforce his own position of strength.

And in this semi-final O'Sullivan was the latest to feel the heat as the players emerged for the much-anticipated showdown on the single table in the Crucible.

Hendry began proceedings with a break of 126, and swiftly followed that up with further runs of 82 and 86. After three frames Hendry led 3-0, had reeled off 295 points without reply, and O'Sullivan had yet to score so much as a single point. The signs were ominous.

Hendry says: "I remember beginning the match with a 126 and that was something I tried to do, and actually did quite a lot when I was playing well and focused – start strongly with a big break, trying to stamp my authority on the match. It was important to get first blood, even in a long match.

"As soon as you lose the tempo it can be hard to get it back, even in a long match."

But O'Sullivan refused to crumble under the onslaught, and could actually have been much better off than 6-2 down after the first session, having had chances in all of the next five frames.

In the second session, however, he hit Hendry with a four-frame blast of his own, including breaks of 67, 122 and 135, levelling first at 6-6 and then 7-7 before Hendry grabbed the last two frames of the day to lead 9-7 overnight.

The scene was set, and the battle royal that the fans had craved exploded into life in the third session on the Saturday morning. With both players at or near the absolute peak of their form Hendry made breaks of 104, 101 and 108, O'Sullivan responded with 81, 84, a 134 that saw him just miss out on another Crucible maximum break and the small matter of £167,000 by missing the final pink, and then a run of 110.

When the dust settled, the pair were all square at 12-12, teeing up the prospect of a titanic final session on the Saturday night.

Clive Everton, commentating for the BBC, intoned as the players walked off: "Hendry went two ahead with two centuries, O'Sullivan levelled with two of his own. This one has been absolutely terrific – snooker from the gods."

Hendry says: "Probably the thing I remember most about that semi-final, apart from actually winning, was the burst of four centuries in a row in the third session.

"That was what Ronnie and I could produce when we were both playing well at the same time. I had breaks of 101 and 108 I think to go 12-10 up, and then he almost made a maximum, missing the last pink, but came back out and got a 110 in the next to level it up at 12-12.

"It feels great to play in a match when you are producing that level with so much at stake, and it must have been good to watch for the crowd and the TV audience."

O'Sullivan adds: "I stayed with him in that match pretty much all the way through, and I started to think that I had a real chance of winning.

"I was playing really well and the moment when I began I think I had what it would take to beat Stephen was in frame 23 when I was on the 147 but missed the pink. I didn't let that fluster me, but came straight back out and made a 110 to level it at 12-12."

Finally, for the first time in the match, O'Sullivan got his nose in front in the first frame of the evening session, making breaks of 44 and 70 to lead 13-12. However, what happened next was to prove something the Rocket would sit, watch, analyse and learn from in the months and years ahead.

If there was a single turning point in the match, it came in frame 26. O'Sullivan, having won the last three frames, was well set and on a break of 32, taking on a straightforward red with the rest. But perhaps thinking too far ahead or taking it for granted, he missed it by a distance, foregoing a great opportunity of a 14-12 lead and seeing the momentum swing decisively in Hendry's favour.

O'Sullivan admits: "I made it 13-12 in the next but one of the big turning points for me was missing a red with the rest in the next frame when I was well set, and could have gone two ahead after being 12-10 down.

"These moments are so huge, because after that I hardly saw a ball. He cleared up to win that frame and make it 13-13, as was his trademark.

"And then I got frozen out, just didn't get a look-in as he won the last five frames. He didn't make any centuries, a couple of 70s and an 80, but he just potted everything.

"But that final session of this match was a huge turning point in my career. At 13-12 up and with the frame at my mercy, I thought, 'I have got him here.'

"Then I missed that red with the rest on 32, I got nervous and he just got stronger and more and more aggressive, more attacking and more dangerous while I was going in to my shell.

"And I came away from that session knowing that if I was going to win a world title, which I hadn't at that time, and major titles I had to find a bit more. I had to go into final sessions and be even more aggressive, and grab matches by the horns exactly as Stephen did in this match.

"It changed me, they often say you learn more from a defeat than a victory. He had done it to me in the past, but this was the Crucible and I knew I had to learn to thrive on the pressure as he did in this arena. If I didn't do that then I was always going to be the bridesmaid because this is where world champions were made – in the final session at the Crucible.

"I had played pretty well but lost, and it was just that extra aggression that I was going to need to hopefully bring me world titles. I think I had to play like that to thrive, whereas others could do it another way, like Mark Selby now. So Stephen had given me the template in this match and I followed it, and it didn't do me any harm.

"My belief wasn't crushed at all, not in any way. I thought I can stay with him at the Crucible, great as he is, I just have to change things slightly to beat him. In recent years you'd compare it to Mo Farah on the track, staying with him is one thing, beating him on the final lap is quite another.

"Basically he played that final session like it was the first frame, and that calmness is what I needed, producing your best in that cauldron."

Hendry not only cleared up with 75 to level at 13-13, but then kept O'Sullivan in the long grass for almost all of the next four frames, concluding victory with a break of 86.

He says: "In long matches it is all about momentum. I did have an early lead of 6-1 but the momentum can change quite easily in a match of four sessions, especially against someone like Ronnie, an inspirational player who can reel off frames in the blink of an eye. And he did that, to get 13-12 ahead.

"The first and last sessions of the long matches, the four-session matches, were generally strengths for me at the Crucible. You tried to win every session, of course, but those could be key. When the chips were down in the last session, usually – not always – I had enough to pull clear.

"And in this match against Ronnie he didn't have much to go at from 13-13 after I levelled it, and I was able to win the last five frames, doing what I liked to do and what I often did."

The job was not quite yet done of course for Hendry, who now had to negotiate another of the famous class of 1992, Mark Williams, in the final. And he duly recorded an 18-11 victory to give him the record seventh world title he had yearned for.

Hendry says: "Beating Ronnie was great, but in the back of my mind was always 'Seven' so I knew I still had a job to do going in to the final against Mark Williams.

"He was an excellent player, and would go on to win world titles himself, and I could not afford to think the hard work was done because it wasn't.

"It really didn't matter who I was playing in that final because all my focus was on getting the seventh, tricky as that was because we were good friends. His nature is to have a joke with you in the corridor, but I was desperate to stay 100 per cent focused and tried to ignore it to get what I really wanted."

For all O'Sullivan's ability, and for all the hype surrounding his inevitable coronation one day as world champion, this defeat left traces of doubt in the Rocket's make-up. While he fully expected to lift the trophy in the near future – and as history shows, he wouldn't have to wait long – at that time he had seen John Higgins scale the Crucible summit, and Mark Williams reach a world final, neither of which he had yet managed to accomplish.

He says: "I did back myself and expected to win it one day. But you did just start to think that Stephen Hendry clearly wasn't going anywhere, he was a force still to be reckoned with.

"And then obviously you had John Higgins who had already won a world title the previous year, with Mark Williams looking likely and then going on to win one in 2000.

"And there certainly was a spell where I began to think, 'Well, why haven't I done it yet?' Each year got harder and harder, and I admit there was doubt starting to creep in."

By 2001 O'Sullivan was finally a world champion – and some of the extra steel to get himself there was drawn from this semi-final defeat to Hendry, and seeing how another of the sport's legends cast pressure aside and accelerated away over the winning line.

Chapter 11

Peter Ebdon v Stephen Hendry, 2002, final

"As an animal, Stephen would have been the baddest, meanest Great White Shark ever because he was ferocious – a killing machine on the table, showing no emotion"

S TEPHEN Hendry may have thought he had done the hard work coming through one grudge clash in the semi-finals of the 2002 World Championship – as it turned out, the victory over Ronnie O'Sullivan to reach a ninth Crucible final merely landed him in another against Peter Ebdon.

The Scot remained the 'King of the Crucible' following his seven world title triumphs achieved in the 1990s but the 'Hendry the Eighth' headlines were still on hold, with Mark Williams and Ronnie O'Sullivan having joined the roster of winners in 2000 and 2001.

However, this year in Sheffield Hendry looked to have given himself an excellent chance of extending his own record haul after emerging intact from an encounter with the Rocket that was dripping with bad blood. O'Sullivan had said in the build-up, among other things, that he looked forward to "sending Hendry back up to his sad little life in Scotland", remarks he was to have rammed back down his throat as the Scot chalked up a third Crucible win over his rival.

Such had been the attention on the clash with defending champion O'Sullivan that it felt like a final, and Hendry by his own admission was not immune to those sentiments. But of course, it was not the final.

Waiting for Hendry in the showpiece was the 31-year-old Ebdon, whom he had beaten with a degree of comfort in the 1996 final to claim world title number six.

But after the intense strain placed both on his emotions and playing resources before and during the O'Sullivan match, Ebdon was probably the last person Hendry needed to be facing – even if that was not how he actually felt heading in to the encounter.

Ebdon was, and remains, something of a snooker one-off. His reputation for off-the-scale intensity and slow play was well deserved, but to dismiss him as simply a tortoise of the baize would be grossly unfair.

The Londoner, who moved to Northamptonshire early in his life, could play all the attacking shots as well as anyone – it just often took him longer to play them. Allied to a superior tactical nous and snooker brain, and fierce will to win, it made him a formidable opponent. He could play all right, and by 2002 had already won four ranking titles.

In the conservative world of snooker Ebdon sported a ponytail for his World Championship debut in 1992, and as his career progressed gave vent to his emotions in the arena around the table in a way that left some his fellow professionals wondering whether these were indeed spontaneous outbursts, or intended to put them off.

Ebdon was also a cerebral individual with academic inclinations and with a musical background that saw him playing the oboe as a youngster, and in 1996 singing on a released single – a cover version of the David Cassidy song 'I Am A Clown'.

But with specific reference to Hendry there was real edge to their matches, for the most part won by the Scot, stemming from at least two separate incidents. When taking on the world No.1 in Dubai in 1992 Ebdon advised his more illustrious rival to "bring his golf clubs, as he won't be playing much snooker". Hendry won the match 5-2.

And then at the 1995 Masters Hendry was irked as Ebdon roared out in triumph while clearing up in the decider before the winning ball was potted for a 5-4 victory.

Hendry knew that Ebdon had the capacity to get under other players' skin, even one as experienced as him – and was also aware that his own mindset was perhaps not quite what it should have been for this final.

He says: "Peter probably emerged as a character when he turned up at the World Championship with a ponytail, I do remember that.

"And one that always stuck in my mind was at the Masters at Wembley against me, I think maybe in 1995, when he potted the brown against me in the decider and went absolutely mental. He still needed the blue to win the match.

"He went on to win, and when you are sat in your chair you don't like that. I suppose when you compare to tennis, they do fist-pumps after every point so maybe we should cope with it better. But in our sport for so many years it wasn't the done thing.

"So when Peter started doing it the other players were a bit like, 'Who's this idiot, and who does he think he is?' If you did those fist-pumps, you got the piss taken out of you by other players.

"Snooker has generally been more reserved, and the cut-loose type of celebration kept for winning the actual tournament. So when Peter started doing it, like in tennis where it can be every shot, it did shake things up a bit.

"He was therefore a completely different character to those that had gone before, and definitely ruffled a few feathers. Players didn't even know him as a bloke or a person, they just asked who is this guy with a ponytail first-pumping all the time?

"My record against him though was very good up until losing that final. I had lost that match in the Benson & Hedges Masters, but apart from that I can't remember losing many important ones to him.

"It was the year when I beat Ronnie in the semi-final when he did all that stuff in the press about me before it, wanting to send me back to my sad little life or whatever it was.

"So there had been a huge build-up to that match and that was a massive match for me psychologically and mentally.

"I wouldn't say I was tired or had nothing left though, I don't agree with that when you are talking about the final of the World Championship. That's the whole point, it's a test, you have to be strong to come through it.

"If you are not up for it, you don't deserve it. That's what the long matches are, a test of stamina, will, temperament, everything. If you don't have those, you won't win it.

"But I came through that one against Ronnie and basically that felt like the final. And subconsciously or even consciously, I thought there is no way Peter can beat me over four sessions.

"Did I actually disrespect him? I'm not sure. But I certainly didn't have the right attitude for that match, the one I normally had. I didn't regroup properly and refocus on the final."

"I did have a slight advantage in that my semi-final finished on the Saturday afternoon, while Peter beat Matthew Stevens 17-16 on the Saturday night.

"Really Matthew Stevens should have beaten him, and from watching some of that match I was expecting to play Matthew the way he had been playing.

"Peter came through and if anyone was struggling to regroup it should have been him, but he was in the final again and had never won it before, nothing to lose in a massive occasion.

"I had beaten him emphatically in 1996 to win the sixth world title, I was confident – maybe over-confident. I just thought the winner of our semi-final would win it before they started."

Ebdon admits that he had emerged from the snooker doldrums that season, leaving him in the correct mental state to launch a serious assault on the World Championship. And having somehow come through a titanic semi-final against Matthew Stevens, winning 17-16 after having the kitchen sink thrown at him by the Welshman, he felt ready to take on the man he called the 'Great White Shark'.

He says: "I was getting pretty fed up of getting beat despite all the hard work. I remember hearing Shaun Murphy saying once he was seriously considering giving it up after a difficult few years, and that was a bit how I felt at times that season.

"But I reached a point where you get introduced to your alter ego – the person you can become if you dig a little deeper. In most of the reading I had done on the psychological side it was thought that a person's greatest success can be one step after their greatest disappointment or failure providing that they use the learning experience.

"And that's what I did, and arrived at the World Championship in great nick, and I knew in my heart I had a great chance of being world champion.

"It doesn't get as much attention but the semi-final against Matthew was an incredible match, I have no idea how I won that one. He threw everything at me, I think it was 17 breaks of 50 or more from him, and I won 17-16 from 16-14 down.

"It is a World Championship final, so of course you want to win – but I wanted it very badly, and just felt very confident, even though I had lost the 1996 final to Stephen.

"I am sure there is a part of Stephen that felt all he had to do was turn up and he would win, with all his experience. And that was certainly a factor in 1996, when I wasn't ready for it. But this time I knew I was ready.

"But that is the beauty of competitive sport. He may have thought all he had to do was turn up, but for me there was absolutely no way that I was going to lose that match. We both believed 100 per cent we would win.

"If I could imagine Stephen in the form of an animal, he would be the biggest, baddest, meanest Great White Shark ever because he was ferocious, a killing machine on the table and just showed no emotion, cold as ice. He battered people, and expected to.

"You could be 4-0 down to him in a final and have done nothing wrong, he'd drop a long red in and clear up so often. And in his mind I'm sure he believed that some of his opponents did not deserve to be at the same table. More often than not, he was right."

Hendry's fears that he might have slipped into over-confidence mode and taken the challenge of Ebdon too lightly were swiftly confirmed, as the contender surged into a 4-0 lead, helped by breaks of 65 and 100 – though the Scot responded in kind, levelling at 4-4 by the end of the first session and knocking in two century breaks of his own.

Ebdon took charge in the second session after a 134 in the first frame of the Sunday night, extending that 5-4 advantage to 10-6 overnight. But Hendry hit back on the afternoon of the Bank Holiday Monday, levelling at 12-12 helped by breaks of 104, 108, 68 and 93, and sure in his own mind once again that an eighth title was within his grasp.

Hendry says: "It is only when he wins the first four frames of the final that you start to think, 'I haven't prepared properly here, I am not focused.' And even in a long match, if your focus is not right from the start, it can be difficult to get it back to where it should be.

"I know you have to be on it from the start, and I have often walked out and stamped my authority on a match from the start, with a century or a big break in the first frame. But that did not happen here.

"And I was constantly chasing on that first day. I got it back to 4-4 in the afternoon, and in the night session I became incredibly frustrated at what I saw as an incredible run of the balls for Peter. Normally if I am focused I am never bothered about that in a long match.

"You won't have heard me talk about bad luck much in my career, or Ronnie O'Sullivan. There is no point, and nothing worse. But in this match, because of my poor mindset and concentration, it was bothering me.

"And that was a very hard session, which I lost 6-2 to be 10-6 down overnight. And given that I was very pleased to get it back to

12-12 after the third session, and I absolutely expected to win again at that point, probably getting ahead of myself."

Coming out for the evening session Hendry got off to a flier, winning the first two frames to move 14-12 ahead at a vital stage, and a situation that Ebdon recognised as requiring an immediate response.

He says: "The pressure at 14-12 down was already unbelievable and winning those next two frames, the first with a century, was the pivotal stage of the match when it could easily have got away from me. I knew what Stephen usually did in this situation and that I had to win those two frames, which fortunately I did."

From 14-14 there was never to be more than a single frame in it, but at 17-16 Ebdon found himself with the prize finally at his mercy. Leading 52-27 there were just two reds left – but Ebdon missed a simple black off the spot, allowing Hendry to sprint to the table. Ebdon, having leapt in the air as the black failed to drop, slumped in his chair shaking his head as Hendry mopped up to force the decider.

But to his credit and as he had to, Ebdon regrouped amid the unbearable tension and after a couple of thrashes where he was fortunate not to leave Hendry with anything easier he took advantage of a missed long blue from the Scot for the break of 59 that was to prove enough.

Hendry was devastated. He says: "Perhaps I was feeling over-confident again. It all became a blur until 17-16 when Peter missed a black off the spot you'd have got with your eyes shut effectively for the title, and I leapt out of my chair to clear up and force a final frame.

"The old cliché, you just want one good chance. He had a couple of goes from distance, could have left me easy ones but didn't, and then made a good break to take charge and I couldn't save myself.

"Even at 17-17 I was so confident, especially the way he had lost the one before. So you have to give credit to him after missing a black off the spot like that almost for the title, to come back and hold himself together for a crucial break.

"I never viewed Peter as a player of the same standard as me, so when a player is sticking with you it is a very bitter pill to swallow. I really, really suffered after that final, and even now years later I feel it is one that slipped away.

"It is right up there with my very worst moments at the Crucible – in fact I am pretty sure it is the worst. Worse than Ronnie beating me big in a semi-final, that doesn't even register by comparison because you know you were outplayed.

"But this, a final you think you should have won, is different. The Ken Doherty final in 1997 where again I felt I should have beaten him over four sessions; this one, and the Steve James quarter-final in 1991 when I was trying to defend were the three worst."

But for Ebdon, this was everything he had worked and sweated for his entire life, and worth the nerve-shredding ordeal of those final two frames.

"It was horrible, missing a black off the spot at 17-16 when I was black, red, black away from winning 18-16 and being world champion. I might have put some unintentional side on it, but when I hit it I thought it was in.

"I jumped up in the air, involuntarily, I had no control over my limbs but I was so shocked the black was still on the table and Stephen cleared up to make it 17-17.

"So I had missed a great chance to win, and all I could do was dig even deeper in the decider. I asked myself for more, it's something I did and happily I found more.

"I potted a really difficult cut red into the middle pocket, dropping it in dead weight and finishing on the pink for a 59 break that pretty much got me there.

"In the final frame my mouth had never been that dry, and it was an amazing feeling to come through and win. It was one of the few finals to go the distance and in its own way a great match, full of drama and tension.

"I know my ex-manager Keith Warren said he would have hated to have seen me had I lost, luckily for both of us we never found out."

Both players were left with their thoughts and reflections after what had been a momentous final, only the third in Crucible history to go the distance.

The extreme disappointment felt by Hendry perhaps also carried a sense within that he would never reach another Crucible final and get another chance to win his eighth world title – and so it was to prove.

He adds: "The World Championship is the biggest and last event, so it is all magnified. The year I lost to Steve James I won about six events, so it had been a great season, but I felt it was a washout because of that result. The Crucible was so important.

"It is still making me annoyed just talking about it now! And this Peter one was the same, you were left with a horrible feeling that you had thrown away a World Championship.

"It is possible to be miserable for months if it is important enough. And there are the continual reminders afterwards, people asking you about it, and mentioning it.

"I get on fine with Peter now, we don't see each other socially a lot and don't have loads in common but we do work together for the BBC sometimes. Having said that, we have never spoken about that final since!"

For Ebdon as for so many champions, being able to share the moment with close family made it all the more memorable and special, as he was joined in the arena by daughter Clarissa and then-wife Deborah.

He says: "I remember Steve Davis coming up to me about 3am at the after-party and saying, 'You should be pissed by now,' but I just knew I wanted to take it all in and remember it.

"Having my family and friends there made it very special, including my dad Michael who is no longer with us sadly. The photographs with him and the trophy the day after are ones I treasure.

"I didn't see him emotional very often, unlike me who is a lot more wear your heart on the sleeve – but even he was that night."

Chapter 12

Paul Hunter v Ken Doherty, 2003, semi-final

"Paul must have been as low as a player can get that day – but he still came up to me and said 'I hope you win it' which was such a generous gesture and showed the person he was"

IN the build-up to the 2003 World Championship there was a press day at London's Groucho Club, a trendy hangout popular with showbiz, media and actor types, and famously featuring a snooker table on the top floor, where if legend has it correctly 'luvvie' luminaries such as Keith Allen played some truly chaotic matches.

And it was here that I and other journalists enjoyed half-hour one-on-one interviews with Paul Hunter – a young player from Leeds who had already made plenty of waves in the sport, but one that was now desperate to prove himself on the biggest stage at the Crucible Theatre.

Twice a winner of the Masters by that point and also with two Welsh Open wins, Hunter brought to snooker an attacking game that was easy on the eye, a ready charm with opponents, fans and media, and a dash of glamour to proceedings that the game badly needed at that time, over-reliant as it was on Ronnie O'Sullivan for headlines.

The British tabloid press fell in love with Hunter after his first Masters win in 2001 against Ireland's Fergal O'Brien, when after completing a stunning comeback for a 10-9 win he revealed that at 6-2 down at the interval he decided to switch to the now infamous 'Plan B' to perk up his fortunes – a strategy that involved then girlfriend and later wife Lindsey Fell back at the hotel.

But on this spring day in the West End, Hunter's mind was very much on another job – attempting to become world champion for the first time.

At that time I was on the staff at the *Daily Express*, and in that newspaper on 18 April Hunter said, from the above interview: "I really look forward to the World Championship, there is so much history at the Crucible. It might not happen for me this year but I will give it my best shot. I just like going down the M1 and seeing the signs to Sheffield, it gives me a huge buzz. The Crucible is where you are judged, normally the better players come through over the longer distance. It is why I get out of bed in the morning, to practise to win the World Championship. I don't think I'd be happy with my career if I never won it, and I'd rather be world champion than world No.1."

As it turned out, the boy from the council estate in Yorkshire increasingly being dubbed the 'Beckham of the Baize' in a reference to the superstar Manchester United and England footballer, would come very close that year.

In the first round be beat Ali Carter 10-5, followed by a 13-6 win over close friend and stablemate Matthew Stevens, also managed by Brandon Parker. Then came a battling 13-12 win over Peter Ebdon in a match that had swung first one way and then the other throughout, and Hunter was into a first World Championship semi-final.

John Spencer and John Pulman battle it out in a semi-final of the 1977 World Championship, the first to be staged at the Crucible Theatre

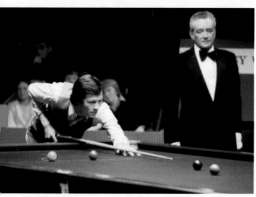

Alex 'Hurricane' Higgins in action against Canada's Cliff Thorburn during their 1980 final

Cliff Thorburn at the table with referee John Street watching on during the 1980 final against Alex Higgins

Cliff Thorburn celebrates with the trophy after his 18-16 victory over Alex Higgins in the 1980 final

Steve Davis in trouble against Tony Knowles as he was throughout their 1982 first-round match, resulting in a sensational 10-1 defeat

Jimmy White and Alex Higgins keep a keen eye on proceedings during their 1982 semi-final

The Whirlwind and the Hurricane produced a semi-final to remember in 1982, with a piece of Alex Higgins magic ultimately turning the tide in his favour

Canada's Cliff Thorburn, alongside good friend Willie Thorne, enjoys the moment after becoming the first player to make a maximum 147 break at the Crucible in 1983

Steve Davis and Dennis Taylor shake hands after the Northern Irishman's dramatic comeback win in the 1985 final

Steve Davis is devastated after losing the 1985 final on the final black to Dennis Taylor

Dennis Taylor kisses the trophy after beating Steve Davis in the dramatic 1985 final

Dennis Taylor offers a consoling handshake to beaten opponent Steve Davis in the immediate aftermath of his stunning 1985 World Championship final victory

Northern Ireland's Dennis Taylor celebrates potting the final black against Steve Davis at 12.19am to win the 1985 world title watched by 18.5million BBC viewers

*(Above, left)
Joe Johnson in
action against
Steve Davis
during the 1986
final*

*(Above, right)
Joe Johnson sings
with his band
Made in Japan
during his run to
the title in 1986*

*Joe Johnson, with
wife Terryl, holds
the trophy aloft
after his stunning
1986 final win
over Steve Davis*

Stephen Hendry in classic pose at the table at the 1992 World Championship, where he claimed title number two

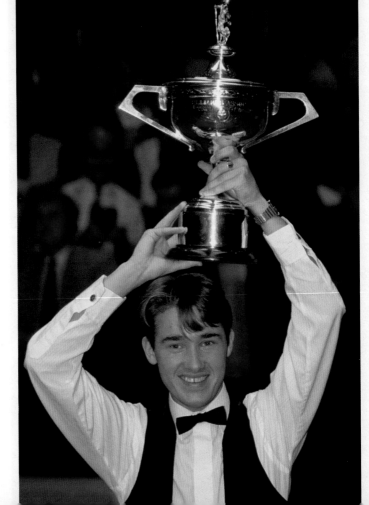

Stephen Hendry holds up the trophy for the crowd and photographers after his 1992 final win over Jimmy White

Stephen Hendry and Jimmy White shake hands before the 1994 final in Sheffield – their fourth in five years

Jimmy White sees his chances of finally winning a world title slip away in the 1994 final against Stephen Hendry

Ronnie O'Sullivan feeling the heat against Stephen Hendry during their 1999 semi-final

Stephen Hendry on a break during his 1999 semi-final in Sheffield against Ronnie O'Sullivan

A determined Peter Ebdon at the table during the 2002 world final against fierce rival Stephen Hendry, a match he went on to win 18-17

Ken Doherty in action against Paul Hunter in their classic 2003 quarter-final – won 17-16 by the Irishman

Matthew Stevens of Wales senses another chance of Crucible glory may be about to slip by during his 2007 quarter-final against Shaun Murphy

Shaun Murphy takes on a pot during his 2007 quarter-final against Matthew Stevens

Steve Davis prepares to walk out into the arena for his last-16 match against John Higgins in 2010

A 52-year-old Steve Davis holds his head in disbelief after beating defending champion John Higgins in their last-16 match

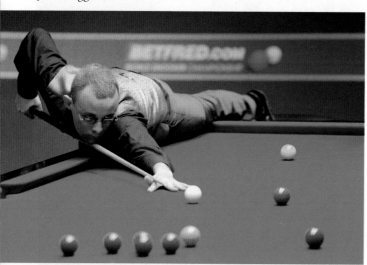

Martin Gould shows the form that took him to the brink of victory against eventual champion Neil Robertson in 2010

Neil Robertson can hardly believe he is through to the quarter-finals after a spectacular comeback win over Martin Gould in 2010

Young guns Judd Trump and Ding Junhui brought the best out of each other in a thrilling semi-final in 2011

Judd Trump celebrates after winning his semi-final against Ding Junhui 17-15 to reach a first world final

The emotions pour out of John Higgins after beating Judd Trump in a superb 2011 final following the toughest year of his life

Judd Trump finally runs out of magic in the 2011 final – finding John Higgins too tough a nut to crack

All smiles once again, Scotland's John Higgins celebrates a fourth world title success with his family in the arena in 2011

A rejuvenated Ronnie O'Sullivan in action during his 2012 quarter-final against Neil Robertson

A disappointed Neil Robertson leaves the arena after losing to Ronnie O'Sullivan in a high-class 2012 quarter-final

There he would meet Ireland's Ken Doherty, the 1997 world champion, and quite simply one of the most canny and wily matchplayers of his generation. Off the table 'Crafty Ken' was and remains as genial as they come – but on it he was a streetfighter.

Doherty, who eventually turned pro in 1990, moved over to England from Ranelagh to develop his game and hone his skills and matchplay. Based in Essex he would take on all comers and practice partners in Ilford, Barking, at Kings Cross in London, and further afield in other hotbeds such as Birmingham, Manchester and Leicester. Ronnie O'Sullivan was later to admit that the beatings he took from Doherty as a youngster helped prepare him for life as a professional.

There were plenty of career highs for Doherty but without question his finest hour came at the Crucible in 1997, beating a then-dominant Stephen Hendry 18-12 to claim the world title. This prompted an outpouring of delirium back home in Dublin, with hundreds of thousands lining the streets to welcome him home with the trophy. And he reached the final again the following year, this time losing by the same scoreline to a youthful John Higgins.

Doherty had taken the hard route to the single-table set-up in 2003, coming through epic matches against Shaun Murphy (10-9), Graeme Dott (13-12) and Higgins (13-8). And though such a doughty competitor and contender for all major titles, Hunter was the slight favourite on form.

Hunter's then manager Parker says: "I did feel that overall at that time Paul was probably the best player in the world. I think he was up to around No.3 or No.4 provisionally and had won the British Open that season and also the two Masters before April 2003.

"And though he did not have a great record at the Crucible at that time, he was playing as well or better than anyone at that time. John Higgins didn't frighten him, he had beaten Stephen Hendry a couple of times, and had a good record against Ronnie, beating him on some big occasions.

"I did feel that whatever the rankings said, this was his time at the Crucible. He was ticking all the boxes, and had the glamour side of it as well as the playing side. I remember Graham Fry of IMG, who produce the BBC coverage, talking to me about Paul that year, and felt he was changing the face of the game.

"Ronnie had his fans, and Jimmy had his fans, both were popular with the geezers, but Paul was attracting new fans to snooker, some completely different people – including women and children. They knew from their viewing figures."

Doherty could have been excused near-exhaustion after his challenging route through the draw, but he was up for another stiff challenge. He recalls: "Going in to the semi-finals I had experience of winning the world title but Paul was one of the best players in the world on current form.

"He had already won the Masters twice, and was becoming a regular contender, and had a great chance of one day becoming world champion.

"I was looking forward to it, and had the knowledge of tough matches under my belt already that year. I was a slight underdog, but I knew I had a good chance, and had that belief.

"But Paul stormed into a 6-2 lead and it just continued like that. One of his greatest assets was that he was cool under pressure and was a good long potter.

"He could win frames very quickly and once he was on a roll it was hard to stop him, you saw that in his wins at the Masters. Even behind, he never flinched.

"At the beginning I just couldn't keep up with him. I tried to play good, tactical snooker and keep him at bay and under pressure, but it wasn't working. He matched or bettered me in every department.

"In the second session I knocked in a couple of good centuries and a 60-odd – but still ended up 11-5 down, and I remember Paul getting a 135.

"So I have to win the third session and probably 6-2 to have a real chance, but even though I steadied the ship we shared those eight frames and it is 15-9 going in to the last session."

Hunter had the bit between his teeth in the first two sessions, and with Doherty needing to make inroads in the third session the Irishman was held at bay. Surely winning eight of the nine remaining frames on Saturday afternoon would prove too stiff a challenge?

But Parker is candid enough to admit that the match situation at that time, positive as it was, handed him another issue on which he has reflected many times since.

He says: "I remember it all vividly, of course. There were two sessions on the Friday after one on Thursday, which meant just one on the Saturday.

"He was 15-9 up after the evening session on the Friday night. And looking back I was a bit upset with myself about some of what went on, and have asked myself if I could have shielded him more.

"I was taking phone calls that Friday night and all the Saturday morning from Paul's family and friends asking about organising rooms for the final.

"And being close to the player I was with him all the time, and he heard some of these calls coming in, from people who had decided he had already won.

"I was trying not to take the calls, but logistically have things covered for all these people calling so as not to risk people being disappointed.

"I should have just turned the phone off and waited for it all to happen, even if it is difficult when it is people you know and you want to try and help them in that eventuality.

"When the families flock down, and you have seen it when Ronnie, John Higgins get to big finals, you have to deal with it all as a manager and I was upset about it afterwards. His father Alan was really good and helped me a lot, but even he was taking call after call at breakfast on the Saturday.

"Paul never, ever mentioned it but little one per cents can be massive and any hint that those around him thought he was already in the final might help an opponent.

"We all know that in snooker if there is the slightest suggestion that you have won something when you haven't, it can come back to bite you. He wasn't over-nervous, but he didn't play well in the final session, not at all. Crafty Ken made a few very scrappy and won all of them."

As it turned out, Parker's fears were well founded. One of Doherty's group of friends had heard provisional arrangements being made about getting all of Hunter's family to the final in the event that he won, and this was duly passed back to the Irishman.

Doherty says: "One of my friends overheard a conversation not involving Paul but within his camp after the third session, with them making arrangements for family and friends to come to the final.

"And it just reminded me at the time of the Cliff Thorburn and Alex Higgins story with the cake that was made for him with the final locked at 16-16.

"If something like that gets back to you, and I'm sure others have said the same about comebacks, it does just gee you up to try and at least create some doubt. It is the kind of thing a football manager might put up on the wall as a team-talk.

"I wasn't angry and it didn't really bother me because I had a huge task already just trying to get back in the match – but I have never been one to tempt fate myself in that way."

It is the nature of sports reporting that often epic contests are distilled down to particular moments. In snooker that can be a brilliant break, a superb shot, some ill fortune or conversely good luck, or a dramatic miss – snapshots that in the context of the encounter significantly shaped the outcome. In this semi-final as the climax neared, a missed yellow from Hunter and a fluked blue from Doherty appeared decisive.

Doherty, who was also trying to make a game of it for some die-hard friends who had arrived from Killarney just in time for the final session, says: "At 15-9 I really didn't think I had much of a chance against a player as good as Paul, and considered the result a foregone conclusion. But as a proud professional you tell yourself to go out and try and win the first frame, and win the first mini-session before the interval to keep the match alive.

"That's all I tried to do, take each frame as it comes – and that is experience. A younger player might have had trouble mentally in that situation, but I didn't fold. In my head I could have given up and been on the flight home. But I couldn't do that anyway! I had four friends who had travelled up from Killarney and then on the boat from Ireland, driving from Holyhead to Sheffield to catch the last session.

"One of the guys was so tired he slept through the whole final session and missed the whole thing, never saw a ball in the arena of one of my greatest wins. But the others were on the balcony cheering me on. I still can't believe he did that though, all the way from Killarney and didn't see a frame.

"But back to the match, I placed a lot of importance on winning that first frame of the afternoon. I wasn't going to hand it to Paul, and was determined to make him win it and work for it.

"I wasn't going to throw it away. And I did win the first frame, and as it turned out the next, then the next – making it five in a row to get back to 15-14.

"And it was the third frame of the afternoon that made me think there could be something in this for me. Paul missed a frame-ball yellow that would have put him 16-11 up.

"He was stretching a little bit, maybe took it a bit too casually and missed the yellow off its spot and that allowed me to nick it on the black to close to 15-12, a huge difference at that stage.

"And I thought 'Wow', knowing that would plant some doubt in his head.

"After making it 15-13 he had 20 minutes at the interval to think about what had happened.

"Although I made it 15-14 he somehow held himself together to make it 16-14. And he could easily have won 17-14 but I fluked a blue with blue, pink and black left on, that was massive.

"It was frame ball for me, left Paul needing a snooker. I had taken the blue on down the rail and fluked it into the middle, it flew in and that was a cruel blow for Paul.

"I just felt that fluke took so much out of him, a real sucker-punch as he had been so close to getting over the winning line in that frame. If I miss the blue and leave it on, he wins. It was a huge slice of luck for me. And I won the last two fairly comfortably. He looked overcome by what had happened."

Had Doherty missed the blue that was frame ball for him and left it on, with pink and black available, there is every chance Hunter would have cleared up to reach a first Crucible final. And the fluke was a crushing blow, as Parker confirms.

"We have all seen how difficult the momentum can be to swap once it shifts, but when Ken got that fluked blue at 16-14, that was horrible," he says.

"You start to really believe in fate being involved in snooker, and when Ken fluked that blue I began to fear it might not be Paul's day, and that this wasn't going to happen.

"There are so many things you remember. The fire alarm had gone off at about 5 or 6am that last morning and we all had to leave the hotel, and stand in the car park for 45 minutes, so that wasn't ideal. And that match was one of the first times the snooker was on BBC One and *Final Score* was swapped on to BBC Two because the viewing figures were so large.

"After the match we decided to go and get pissed and went back to Bredbury Hall, one of his sponsors. It was a good night out.

"But at about 11.30pm a bloke came up to Paul at the bar and said 'Paul, you're doing brilliant, and you're going to win the World Championship this year!'

"Paul gave him a big grin and said, 'Much as I appreciate your support mate...afraid I got beat this afternoon!' By then he was laughing again after a few vodkas."

Speaking straight after the loss, though, Hunter admitted: "I am devastated because this is the best tournament in the world, and it is hard to lose in the semi-finals like that. I knew he would come back at me. I tried to stay positive and I still fancied it when it went to the decider, but it wasn't to be. Hopefully I can come back and win this one day. I have had an excellent season and I can take the positives out of it."

There were consoling words from World Snooker's then chief executive, Richard Relton. He said: "Paul is still only 24. He is a tremendous talent and in addition a good-looking guy, with a bright future and possessing all the attributes needed. Most sports are hoping and praying to find people like Paul, and I see him as one of the key elements in driving the sport forward. Like many people I was gutted for him losing in that manner to Ken."

And after yet another draining match, Doherty's race was run. Even though he recovered from 10-2 down against Mark Williams to take it to 16-16, there was precious little left in the tank and it was the Welshman, rather than the Irishman, who won a second world title.

Doherty says: "It is an amazing feeling to win a match like that one against Paul at the Crucible, especially in the one-table set-up. I was actually a bit overwhelmed and I felt a bit flat for the final.

"I think I was just drained after the semi-final, and some other tough matches. I fell 10-2 down to Mark Williams and although I managed to get close there wasn't much left and I couldn't do it again.

"The efforts had taken their toll, but sport is about moments and the semi-final is one I will never forget. I'm not sure anyone has come back to win from further behind in a best-of-33-frame semi-final."

The following year, after a third sensational Masters success achieved by beating Ronnie O'Sullivan in the final, Hunter acknowledged in the *Daily Express*: "I'm not going to deny it, I was absolutely gutted after losing to Ken in the last year's Crucible semi-final. It is the most hurt I have ever been over a snooker match. But I am already looking forward to going back to Sheffield and the Crucible this year."

Hunter did return in 2004, this time losing to Stevens in the second round – but his next appearance at the World Championship in 2005 was a far more poignant occasion. At just 26 years of age Hunter announced days before heading for the Crucible that he had been diagnosed with malignant neuroendocrine tumours and would require chemotherapy for the rare form of cancer.

The news came as a stunning blow first and foremost for Hunter himself, Lindsey, who he had married in Jamaica in 2004, and the rest of his family and friends – but also the world of snooker, where the player was such a popular figure.

The ovations as he walked out to face good friend Michael Holt were prolonged, heartfelt and deeply moving, and it made for a difficult occasion for either to concentrate, with Nottingham's Holt visibly upset and unable to celebrate in the usual fashion after a 10-6 victory.

Hunter did battle on, playing the following season but his treatment was not allowing him to be the same player. By now a father to daughter Evie Rose, Hunter's final match was against Neil Robertson at the Crucible on 17 April, 2006 and one of snooker's brightest stars passed away in October, a few days short of his 28th birthday.

A husband, father and son was cruelly snatched away, and the hopes and dreams of winning a world title at the Crucible would never be realised. But Hunter left a huge legacy, not least in the form of the excellent charitable and educational work of the Paul Hunter Foundation set up in his name.

Doherty is certain that this semi-final would be remembered as a great match even if Hunter were still alive today, but admits that subsequent events do lend the Leeds player's best ever run at the Crucible extra significance.

He says: "Because of the prize at stake, and his big lead, and the chances he missed and my good luck and all that, Paul must have been as low as a player can get that day. I know, because I would have been.

"But he still came up to me and shook my hand and said, 'Well played and I hope you win it now.' It was such a generous gesture and showed exactly what sort of person Paul was. I really liked the kid, he is still much missed today by those that knew him well and I would have loved him to win a world title.

"At the time I couldn't wait to get into the final and try and win a second world title. But that defeat for him is more poignant now because of happened to Paul, and he could easily have won the title that year. When I reflect on the match it is tinged with sadness.

"Paul played in some great matches both at the Crucible and of course at the Masters where he won it three times.

"He may well have gone on to win a world title, there are no guarantees of course, but very sadly his life was taken way too early and he never got all his chances."

And Parker is in no doubt about how to sum up Hunter as a player, and a person. He says: "He had ice in his veins as a player, and real inner calm – priceless qualities in snooker. The words are overused, but he had them.

"After Paul died Graeme Dott said in one of his tributes that you could walk into a match and see a score of 7-2, and looking at Paul you wouldn't know if he was winning or losing.

"Neil Robertson is similar now, so composed. But Paul was also a real fighter, and one of those players you almost didn't want to be in front of. Arguably he was more dangerous there than when leading, he was a relentless devil when he was chasing.

"He could score, had a good safety game, but it was the composure that marked him out. And as a person I have never met anyone like him – the nicest man I have come across. He treated everyone the same, whether you were the king or a tramp. He was great with fans, and had no airs and graces, and wasn't in any way materialistic.

"People would come up to me and say, 'Do you think he'd let me say hello?' and I'd just say 'Go and speak to him', and they did, often for ten minutes having a drink. He put people at ease.

"In China sometimes we'd be at big formal banquets with some pretty unusual, exotic food and he'd be trying to hide it under the table so as not to cause offence. He came off a council estate, and never forgot where he came from despite all the fame and money."

Hunter's greatest triumphs may have come at the Masters, where the trophy was renamed in his honour for the 2017 staging of the tournament. But at the World Championship and the Crucible, this was the match for which he will be best remembered.

Chapter 13

Ronnie O'Sullivan v Stephen Hendry, 2004, semi-final

"If you have been a bully all of your career, when someone bullies you back it is not a nice feeling"

BY the time of the 2004 World Championship the balance of power between Ronnie O'Sullivan and Stephen Hendry had shifted considerably.

O'Sullivan had of course claimed a first world title in 2001, overdue in the eyes of some but still achieved at the age of only 25, and offering the possibility of plenty more success at the Crucible.

And while Hendry still harboured aspirations of an eighth World Championship success those hopes were starting to fade, having lost in the final two years previously to Peter Ebdon, a defeat that as we have heard cut the Scot to the quick. Earlier in the season Hendry had beaten O'Sullivan 9-6 in the British Open final at the Brighton

Centre to lift what would prove to be his penultimate ranking title trophy – then going on to lose in the UK Championship final 10-8 a fortnight later to Matthew Stevens in York.

Then in the space of a couple of weeks in early 2004 O'Sullivan experienced both sides of deciding-frame finishes in major finals, pipping Steve Davis 9-8 to win the Welsh Open in Cardiff, but losing 10-9 to Paul Hunter in the Masters final at the Wembley Conference Centre.

Both arrived with genuine title aspirations, although O'Sullivan was the favourite with the bookmakers to win a second title three years after his first. And by now the six-time former champion Ray Reardon was in his corner, to bring some craft and matchplay nous to the party to temper some of the Rocket's wilder inclinations at the table.

With the pair seeded two and three and therefore expected to meet for a place in the final O'Sullivan came through the harder first-round match with a 10-6 win over Stephen Maguire, while Hendry dismissed Stuart Pettman 10-2. But both were pushed very hard in their last-16 matches, O'Sullivan eventually easing clear of trouble at 10-9 down to Andy Hicks to win 13-11, while Hendry was given an even bigger scare by Barry Pinches before edging into the quarter-finals 13-12.

But both gave themselves some extra time off before the match the fans, media and television viewers had been craving since day one by winning their quarter-finals with a session to spare, Hendry 13-3 against Ian McCulloch and his rival, particularly impressive against Anthony Hamilton, progressing through the same scoreline.

Quite apart from the long-standing on-table rivalry there was still plenty of edge between the players following O'Sullivan's comments ahead of their semi-final two years previously. On that occasion he had promised to send Hendry "back to his sad little life in Scotland" among other similarly uncomplimentary barbs.

The words were rather rammed back down O'Sullivan's throat as Hendry ran out, as he had in 1999, a 17-13 winner and though the tension had eased slightly the handshake at the start of the semi-final betrayed lingering animosity.

A repentant O'Sullivan recalls: "Obviously we had a couple of semi-finals before this one, including the one in 2002 when I made the comments about Stephen after my quarter-final.

"It affected our relationship badly and really I had no problem with Stephen, but it was a big mistake and I think I probably had been listening too much to Naseem Hamed.

"We were down the gym and he was telling me, 'When you do your press conferences you have got to do this and say that to stir it up a bit.'

"I can be a bit easily led and I thought 'Right then, let's give this a go, I'll do that.' It was like he was telling me to do some boxing-style trash-talking.

"Then when I did it Naz was like, 'Oh no mate, I didn't mean like that, what were you saying, I didn't mean Hendry?' I am not blaming him, it was my fault and shows how impressionable I could be. But I do really regret it, one of my biggest regrets in the game.

"We do get on a lot better now, and I did apologise to Stephen, but maybe it is hard to totally eliminate once you have said it.

"So this match was two years later, and we hadn't spoken for two years and that was difficult on tour. I had created an atmosphere that was no good for either of us. It wasn't great.

"There were little nods only still at that time, so things were a bit tense. It may be okay in boxing but not really in snooker so much, and I am still a bit embarrassed by it."

Hendry admits that he had kept his distance from O'Sullivan on the circuit after the episode in 2002, and that, though diluted, some of the feelings stirred up were taking their time to ebb away.

And looking back he now believes the seeds for his comprehensive defeat may have been sown as long before as 1999 when he won the record seventh world title in Sheffield.

He says: "We had a period where it was pretty tense. After all, basically he said he didn't like me, and how would any of us react to someone saying that?

"He said loads of things but one was 'I've never liked him and only speak to him when I have to' and so you just think well, if they don't like me the sensible thing is to stay away from them.

"I wasn't too bothered about the other stuff about trying to send me back to Scotland. He was egged on by people, and he has told me that many times since but we get on fine now and it was already a bit better by 2004.

"And playing-wise it was a different situation now with Ronnie. He had won a world title, and was the favourite to win it again that year.

"I am told the media were desperate, as they were in 2002, to get the 'King Hendry the Eighth' headlines written but I couldn't be thinking about that with such a tough challenge ahead of me.

"Ronnie had started to show what he could do and was now a proven Crucible winner, and having that knowledge that you can come out of the 17 days on top makes a huge difference to a player's belief and mindset.

"My attitude by 2004 had changed, and whereas in say 1999 I arrived thinking I was the man to beat and expecting to win, that was no longer the case.

"I remember saying after winning the seventh that if I never win another match I am happy. And maybe that was one of the nails in the coffin.

"I would never have said anything like that when I was dominating, and maybe I never should have said it. It sent the wrong messages to everyone, myself included. I was still a professional, still playing, still a top player.

"It almost admits to everyone that I am taking my foot off the gas. It doesn't mean the ability has gone, but maybe some of the intensity and arguably though I won other titles and played some great snooker, I was perhaps never the same player."

The one-table set-up beckoned and the world held its breath as the two titans of the game, widely described as the greatest player in snooker's history in Hendry's case, and the most naturally talented player ever to lift a cue in the case of O'Sullivan, prepared for battle.

It was expected at least one would play to an exceptional standard, and hoped that both might manage it. As it turned out, Hendry simply could not live with a rampant O'Sullivan. In one of his more prophetic moments at the microphone at the start of the first frame, BBC commentator Willie Thorne suggested: "If one of these players plays badly, they are going to get heavily beaten."

At the beginning of the contest, at least, O'Sullivan was feeding off his usual partisan backing in the atmosphere he cherished above all others, hoping to shrug off the additional burdens that came with such a devoted following demanding both victory and entertainment.

He says: "It is the ultimate for me and most players, playing in a big match at the Crucible. It is the World Championship, the biggest tournament, and where you sink or swim.

"It can be the loneliest place, or the best place to play out there on your own. I liken it to Yin and Yang, it can equally be so bad, or fantastic, both sides of the spectrum.

"So much meaning and importance is loaded on to playing well there, by yourself and of course by others, and it has special meaning.

"So when you are flying there, and I have been lucky enough to experience that feeling a few times there including in this match, there is no feeling like it. It is intoxicating.

"I don't really know any different but to have great support at the Crucible, so that is fortunate to have that backing. But with that comes added pressure, and disappointment if you are not performing. You'd almost rather people weren't that upset if you lost.

"I always feel a weight of expectation to deliver, both play well and give value for money. And to use an example from much later, even though I lost to Barry Hawkins in 2016, I felt I played well for most of that match. Maybe if I had got through that I would have won it again, we will never know.

"It is about moments, and that was one where even though I lost I played well, the atmosphere was great, and it was a great match and a good show. I am a winner, but seeing the crowd enjoying it is also very important for me."

And his followers certainly enjoyed themselves for the 21 frames it took to take care of Hendry in this semi-final. From the moment O'Sullivan, sporting a hairband to contain some flowing locks, knocked in first a fine long red and failed to get on a colour, swiftly followed by a break of 85 to clinch the frame, the signs were ominous for Hendry.

The Scot did level at 1-1 with a break of 61, but it needed another of 81 just to peg O'Sullivan back to a 6-2 first-session advantage, which already looked too much to claw back against someone who was usually such a strong front-runner. As it turned out, O'Sullivan had still more gears.

There were further breaks of 127, 67 and 98 in that first session, and then he waged war on Hendry in the second session on the Friday afternoon, removing the last vestiges of his rival's dignity by surging 13-3 in front with breaks of 81, 92, 52, 117, 42, 58 and 63. It was a public savaging, and the only real surprise was that O'Sullivan had not made more century breaks.

He says: "I knew I had to win the semi-final to go to No.1, so that was on it as well but I think I was favourite for the title before the match.

"I had just started working with Ray Reardon coming in to this tournament, and by the semis was feeling I was struggling a bit and had lost a bit of my form.

"Ray just helped me tighten up a bit, against Andy Hicks in the last 16 it was very nip and tuck until I got a bit of advice on the phone and managed to pull away from 10-9 down to win 13-11.

"Ray turned me into a better matchplayer, much more on the percentages.

"And I played a good match against Hendry, although I also remember that he was struggling. And it was going through my mind, 'He is not the same player he was.' In his prime it would have been closer.

"It was an emphatic scoreline, and there was the slight element that he was like a great boxer who had maybe gone on a bit too long, and was past his best.

"So in that sense the balance had shifted by now in my favour, it looked like one-way traffic. If only he had known some of what was going through my mind he might have had more belief in that match!

"It was very one-sided, and when you have as much respect for a player as I had for Stephen, plus the difficulties I had created in the relationship, it almost felt a bit awkward.

"I came in after the second session and it was 13-3, but Ray thought it should have been 14-2 as I had lost the last one, the only one of the session. 'What were you doing playing that shot?' he was saying. 'You should have nailed him.' I thought I was doing pretty well as it was, but that was how he got that extra bit out of me.

"And he was going on at me, 'When you've got them on the ground stamp on their head, and put the concrete on top of them!' I was laughing, saying 'Jesus, Ray!'

"It was brutal stuff.

"It wasn't my natural attitude and maybe that is why I am not like a Ray Reardon, a Stephen Hendry or a Steve Davis. They were evil on the table, no mercy. But quality and entertainment counted more for me.

"There was empathy from me, and had it been the other way around there might not have been any! If he had been 13-2 up he would have wanted to annihilate me but I never thought that against my heroes like Hendry and Davis."

The final rites were at least administered fairly swiftly by O'Sullivan, and he rattled in breaks of 71, 93 and then a finishing flourish of 79 to race through the winning line. Incredibly the handshake at the end, despite the scoreline, was warmer than the one at the beginning.

O'Sullivan was feeling sorry for his rival, Hendry had been on the end of a masterclass.

By the end, it was O'Sullivan's total dominance that was being hailed by the BBC commentary team. John Virgo said: "If you were marking out of ten in every department in this match, Ronnie would be getting maximum points."

Clive Everton, sitting next to Virgo, agreed: "For potting, safety and break-building, also attitude and concentration, it has been relentless Ron."

As the players left the arena with O'Sullivan holding his cue extension aloft, Everton added: "A superlative performance from O'Sullivan, break after break tripped off his cue."

"Poetry in motion," had been Virgo's earlier summation and for once the cliché was not used gratuitously, as a desolate Hendry was left staring at the floor from his chair for such long periods of the encounter.

The fact that the greatest winning margin in Crucible semi-final history had been inflicted on the player who had enjoyed the most success in the venue was a peculiar irony, and a humbling and embarrassing experience for someone who had dished out plenty of such pain to others over the years.

There are plenty of close finishes in this book, and witnessing the drama of a final frame at the Crucible is a unique and adrenaline-filled experience for the spectators, let alone the players. This was no such thing, and probably a controversial choice for that.

Controversial also for the level of Hendry's play. Would he have stood up to this O'Sullivan bombardment in his pomp in the 1990s? That is of course one of sport's great imponderables and we will never know for sure.

My own hunch for what it is worth is that even with a rock-solid safety game and missing little or nothing offered up by the Rocket, neither of which was the case in this semi-final from Hendry, that the 2004 vintage O'Sullivan might still have proved too good. Others will disagree. And for me the whole experience, watching sometimes from the media centre and occasionally from the press seats inside the arena, reminded me of one of the other loves of my sporting life – horseracing.

Prior to this match when I watched Dancing Brave on the flat or Istabraq over hurdles, it wasn't to see a close finish. It was to see these horses show just how good they were, a demonstration of excellence, speed and stamina taking them away from their rivals.

In more recent years it was the same with the legendary Frankel, and over obstacles with the likes of Kauto Star and Sprinter Sacre. You watched to admire, and it was impossible not to admire and appreciate O'Sullivan's performance in this match – and also to acknowledge some symbolic passing on of the torch for good even if seeing Hendry, such a great champion, dismantled in this way made for uncomfortable viewing. Arguably Hendry, already seeing his powers waning, was never the same player again after this loss.

He says: "It was almost as if I had got an excuse in early before the match, when I said we were both capable of beating the other heavily. Like I was expecting something like this could happen, I had laid the foundations.

"He outplayed me, and was the much better player, but essentially you wanted to slink away and not talk about it too much.

"The only consolation was that I wasn't at the peak of my powers, because to lose like that would have been even more devastating.

"It wasn't quite a 'Should I retire' match for me, but one that put major doubts in my mind as to whether I could still compete with the very best players out there on the biggest stages.

"It left scars, no question, about whether I could still compete. And it was more whether I could still match that level. Ronnie had gone up to my previous level or even beyond, and could I maintain that, to compete.

"Arguably there was a slow decline from 1999, and it was highlighted pretty starkly in this match. You don't realise it at the time, but maybe I was so focused on doing something that no one else had done, winning the seven world titles, that pushing on for more was difficult after achieving it."

O'Sullivan would go on to win a second world title by beating Graeme Dott 18-8 in the final, celebrating with a pair of fangs in the arena after so much help from Reardon, the man they used to call Dracula.

He adds: "It was maybe the beginning of the end for Hendry, I'm not sure he totally recovered from that match though he did go on to reach a couple of UK finals I think, and win another ranking title.

"I didn't think that at the time, but maybe now looking back it was. And now I have come to a later stage of my own career I can see how that could happen.

"You start to wonder if you can keep getting up after taking the punishment. If you have been a bully all of your career, when someone bullies you back it is not a nice feeling."

Chapter 14

Ronnie O'Sullivan v Peter Ebdon, 2005, quarter-final

"It was the most painful experience of my snooker career – I was clawing my head in the chair, drawing blood scratching with my nails and I just wanted out of there"

IN terms of the extraordinary spectacle but perhaps even more the bitter and furious fallout, that in one form or another lasted many months, it is hard to think of any match in Crucible history that can top the meeting of Ronnie O'Sullivan and Peter Ebdon as they chased a place in the semi-finals of the 2005 World Championship.

The Rocket arrived in Sheffield off the back of winning a second world title 12 months before, ranked at No.1 in the world, seemingly at the peak of his powers and after tearing it up and exerting his influence all season on the tour – apart from the China Open, missed on medical grounds that saw criticism from other players. There had already been successes at the Grand Prix with a 9-5 win over Ian McCulloch, the Welsh Open with a thrilling 9-8 victory over Stephen Hendry, a 10-3 demolition of John Higgins in the Masters final and a 10-8 win over Matthew Stevens at the Irish Masters, the last time that tournament was staged as a ranking event.

World No.8 Ebdon, the older man at 34 to O'Sullivan's 29, had won six ranking titles including his 2002 World Championship triumph but his season had been unspectacular, the highlight to this point being a Masters semi-final which saw him lose 6-3 to Higgins.

As previously noted Ebdon rejoiced in a reputation for a 'methodical' approach to his matches – invariably playing an attacking shot, or the right shot, but often after lengthy deliberation and addressing of the cue ball. But his all-round game was far too strong for Australian Quinten Hann in the last 32, coming through 10-2, before having to work much harder to beat Stephen Lee 13-9.

By contrast O'Sullivan had only just survived the first round 10-9, having to win the last three frames, after being handed the worst draw imaginable in the form of recently crowned UK Championship winner Stephen Maguire. The last-16 match against Ali Carter was less stressful, yielding a 13-7 win.

So the die was now cast and the Crucible had a supreme 'Hare and Tortoise' clash of styles on its hands as the match got under way in the afternoon on Tuesday, 26 April. The pair had met twice previously at the World Championship, Ebdon winning a semi-final 16-14 in 1996 before O'Sullivan gained a measure of revenge with a 13-6 victory on his way to the title in 2001.

Ebdon was fully aware of the daunting challenge he faced, and also what he would need to bring to the party to have any chance of winning.

He says: "Ronnie had just won his second world title the previous year, and as is often the case all the talk had been about him coming in to the tournament. He was world No.1 at the time and was just playing some amazing stuff; when he was in the mood he looked like he owned that place.

"Every match you play against him, especially at the Crucible, has the potential to be something special but you do have to turn up as his opponent, and put in a performance. And that is easier said than done when the pressure is on at the World Championship.

"You know that even aside from his ability most people want him to win, including a lot of the commentators and people watching at home. So you are not just playing Ronnie, especially at the Crucible, you are playing everyone because they all want you to get beat whoever you are.

"It is all about your own preparation, staying focused and in the zone, and not allowing any distractions to seep in and get to you. There are enough pressures and stresses in snooker as it is, many of which people never get to see.

"Things like whether your tip is okay can be a huge deal, you can be playing well, break your tip, and that form all disappears and your chance has gone. Ronnie is one of the few people who can put on a new tip and play as well or better.

"I have practised with him in the build-up to the World Championship many times, especially since this match, and he can knock in centuries with a new tip like I have never seen. But it is just another example of his gifts, his talent, touch and feel as a snooker player and we all know that as fellow professionals."

O'Sullivan, so relieved to still be alive and kicking, freely admits that Ebdon was not his favourite opponent and was viewing the contest with a sense of dread rather than enthusiasm over the possibilities that victory afforded. And at that time he lacked the coping mechanisms when bored, disinterested or out of form that would eventually be handed to him by sports psychiatrist Steve Peters, more of whom in a later chapter.

O'Sullivan says: "Stephen Maguire was about as tough a draw as I could have had in the first round, probably the hardest first-round draw in history. He had of course just won the UK that season, was set to shoot up the rankings and I was lucky to beat him.

"Stephen had won tournaments, got to the semis in Brighton as well that season, and no one wanted him. I started to think it was being rigged after getting Maguire again, and Fu the year before that.

"I was still in, but I never enjoyed playing Peter because he never knew when he was beaten. I remember playing him in an exhibition once, where you are supposed to relax and enjoy your shots, and even there he sweated a pint of blood over every shot.

"So I knew this geezer fights to the end, and he wanted it like almost no one you had seen, and would give everything to win. It made me think sometimes, 'Can you want it too much?'"

The ability never to give up is an attribute required by any sportsperson, and if you were creating a composite snooker player, it was this level of determination that Ebdon would contribute. At times the fierce self-belief can appear almost delusional, but that is how many top professionals keep the doubts at bay, and the type of uncertainty that can see a player unravel.

He recalls: "We are all human and sometimes we don't turn up as sportspeople on a given day. You just hope it isn't one of the big ones, and do all you can to stop that happening. And you can't give up, if things aren't going well you have to relax, regroup and go again.

"Trying new things can work, or it can backfire. But I have always found that trying to relax can help me get it back. There is no magic switch, and lots of different techniques. I have worked with people like Steve Sylvester and Chris Henry in the area of sports psychology, and people close to you can see things you can't see yourself in the heat of battle.

"Hopefully I have done something similar for Ali Carter since. But playing Ronnie everything has to be spot on. Not only do you have to be a very good player, but if you do happen to catch him on an off day and get chances, you must take them and step up to the plate.

"Not everyone can do that against great champions like Hendry or Davis, it can be hard. These players had an aura of invincibility, and it could be very difficult to come back once they were ahead, they were great front-runners. And that aspect was the most pleasing thing for me in this match."

Ebdon did indeed have to dig deep as O'Sullivan showed those front-running qualities. He stormed into a 6-2 lead after the first session, helped by breaks of 71, 137, 101, 79 and 71 – and then claimed the first two frames of the second session with runs of 60 and 54. It was now 8-2, and the bookmakers were ready to pay out on a player who had been a strong favourite at the start.

But all of a sudden, Ebdon managed to slow the O'Sullivan juggernaut down and the Rocket, failing to deal with the pace of play and prolonged tactical exchanges, came off the boil. Ebdon became slower and slower, and O'Sullivan became more and more frustrated.

That the 2002 champion played much of this match at a speed that would have had a snail up in arms is not in question, and the crowd in the arena remained gripped by the mental battle even if the encounter was a long way from a free-flowing shootout. The key questions put to Ebdon afterwards were whether he had done it deliberately to put off his opponent, or was he simply caught up in an intense world of his own, desperately trying to regain a foothold in the match.

Either way, at that time this was O'Sullivan's idea of snooker hell, and he was suffering – and not just because the lead was slipping away.

O'Sullivan, the game's great entertainer at that time, says: "Maybe there is a threshold where it becomes unattractive to watch. And in that match I felt his tactics were designed to bring the worst out in me. For me it was probably within the rules of the sport, and part of the sport, but it is not how I would want to be remembered as a snooker player winning a match."

"As good as Maguire was, him and Ali Carter in the last 16 suited my game, they tried to have a go and that was okay. But if I was not feeling like the game is coming easy to me then someone like Ebdon, who puts the balls all scrappy and on the cushions and takes ages, could get to me.

"And at that time, before the days of Steve Peters, I felt as if I didn't have the patience to be there all day over three sessions, five hours a session. It wasn't THAT important to me, as it was to Peter. I wanted to be involved in good games, and at that time if they weren't, I struggled.

"I was 8-2 on Peter and was wondering out there at the time, 'How am I 8-2 up here playing like this?' I hadn't played that well, despite a couple of centuries. And then it just got slower and slower, and every ounce of what I needed to win the match had left me. I knew I just couldn't stick it, and wanted out of there.

"Who knows, maybe if I had been working with someone who could help me through it in 2005, things might have been different. Even if I hadn't have won, I might not have imploded like I did, and managed my emotions better. I needed things to fall back on for what happened, and I didn't have them then."

It was, as O'Sullivan says, an implosion – a spectacular meltdown of epic proportions. Ebdon, who famously referred to O'Sullivan as snooker's Mozart some years previously, gradually clawed his way back, and finished the second session four frames adrift at 10-6 having started to get a few wrong notes out of his opponent.

In the next frame, the first of the Wednesday evening and final session, came one of the two most talked-about moments of the match. Ebdon led 22-0 and O'Sullivan had left the cue ball tight on the top cushion with reds spread all over the table, and a difficult safety shot ahead.

Difficult, but perhaps not worthy of the three minutes Ebdon spent deliberating over what to do. He eventually played off a red in baulk, was lucky not to leave O'Sullivan an easy opening, and went on to win the frame and close the gap to 10-7.

And then in frame 20, the fourth in a streak of six that Ebdon was to win, came arguably the most famous break of 12 in snooker history. Ebdon took fully five minutes and 40 seconds to pot red, blue, red, blue, and miss the next red before returning to his chair.

O'Sullivan, who had been asking members of the crowd the time, could not stop laughing as his opponent returned to his chair. He of course had made a maximum 147 break in just five minutes and 20 seconds eight years earlier against Mick Price. And from 12-10 down, despite winning the next, the game looked up for O'Sullivan as he eventually lost 13-11.

Ebdon says: "I didn't play particularly well, but I was so determined to come back and win that will go down as one of my greatest wins. It was special to me, because I wanted it so badly and I took absolutely everything he had to throw at me in the early part of the match. I don't think anyone could have played much better than he did early on, and he was well clear.

"But I managed to get calm, use my deep inner self-belief, and just say 'Right, okay, that's fine, he's done that but let's take it one frame at a time and I can do this.' I never discounted myself from winning that match at any time. I find if I have prepared properly, it helps my belief. And then you call on those other things you may have, desire, determination and the rest. They were my edge."

By the end, O'Sullivan just wanted the suffering to end – win, lose, whichever way was quicker. He says: "There is something on YouTube where they split the screen and show my Crucible maximum from 1997, in quite a bit less time than he took for that break of 12 – red blue red blue.

"I don't know whether he was so engrossed he wasn't aware of what he was doing, or whether he was totally aware. I'd like to think it was the former, and put him on a lie detector test! I remember asking people in the crowd the time, and finding the break of 12 quite funny. I was thinking we were going to be there until 1am.

"I had had a haircut, a crew cut to try and make myself feel better before the final session and I was clawing my head in the chair, I drew blood scratching my head with my nails!

"I just wanted out of there, I knew I couldn't march through him and from early on in the final session. I knew I just had to take the pain. I accepted another world title wasn't coming, and just wanted to get as far away from Sheffield as possible.

"It was THE most painful experience of my snooker career – that and the semi-final against Graeme Dott the year after when I kept on having to change my tip. The two worst experiences I have ever had in the game.

"There was a huge reaction from the media and TV viewers afterwards. Personally I was just relieved it was over. The next morning I said to him, 'Well done and good luck, I know how important it is to you, you've got to do what you've got to do,' he had his wife with him. But I was so relieved to be going home.

"People were saying it was a liberty and things, and Hazel Irvine on the BBC put some awkward question to him in the studio and he started crying. Perhaps the fact it was against me just made it higher profile."

The aftermath was certainly almost as dramatic as what had happened on the table. Right from the off Ebdon became aware of the disapproval, with angry viewers having bombarded the BBC about the spectacle they had witnessed.

And his defence of the way he played was to end up in court, as he unsuccessfully tried to sue columnist Matthew Syed and *The Times* for suggesting that Ebdon had played so deliberately slowly to put off his opponent that his actions constituted cheating. The case went to binding arbitration in order to try and minimise the costs arising from a full defamation trial, and the judge found that Syed's opinion was fairly held based on the arguments and evidence he had put forward. The fact Syed was a columnist, there to provide opinion and comment rather than straight reporting, was a big factor in the case.

Ebdon says: "For me the huge disappointment was what happened after the match and some of the stuff that went on in the press that hurt. Basically I sued *The Times* newspaper over an article written by Matthew Syed, that basically said I had cheated and deliberately played slowly to put Ronnie off. It was totally out of order at the time, and in my opinion it remains so today.

"Matthew Syed, who was a sportsperson himself, was saying a fellow sportsperson had cheated and I just thought he crossed a line with that piece and there was absolutely no way once that was said that I wasn't going to sue, even if I lost.

"In the end the process ended up going down some kind of arbitration route and I lost that arbitration on the grounds that it was a comment piece and not a factual piece.

"I ended up having to pay the disbursements though I had gone in as a no-win, no-fee. My solicitor had been very confident we would win that case, obviously it was all new to me.

"And I was absolutely devastated that what I regarded as one of my greatest wins ended up being overshadowed for some people by these allegations against me. Even when I walked into the TV studio afterwards, Hazel [Irvine] was there. I thought they were going to say 'Wow, what an amazing comeback, you must be over the moon.'

"And instead I was hit with, 'We have had complaints from viewers all over the place about how slow you were.' I couldn't understand it, I had come back from 8-2 down against Ronnie, giving it everything I had to do that.

"The referee Colin Brinded came in for some criticism for not getting involved more during the match. There were even suggestions in the press that the fact I was a member of the board of the governing body could give rise to a perceived conflict of interest. Very sadly, he died within months.

"I just felt it was really, really unfair some of that was said. I am a professional sportsman and I was trying my hardest. Some people just don't like it when Ronnie gets beat. Without a doubt you get this bitterness coming out when the result doesn't go the way people want. I mean look at social media these days, if people lose bets.

"And it goes back to what I said earlier about playing everyone when you play Ronnie. I wish commentators were made to listen back to what they say, there is often an inherent bias towards and against certain players. Everyone wants Ronnie to win and produce his magic.

"And genuinely I am his biggest fan, I love watching it too. Look how he played in those two finals against Ali Carter, Ali never had a chance really. Many players look like rabbits caught in the headlights against Ronnie, and yet if you fight and stand your ground you are a cheat?"

Chapter 15

Matthew Stevens v Shaun Murphy, 2007, quarter-final

"When you are young you have no battle scars —
the damaging defeats, ones that really hurt and
with what had happened two years before in the
final there was some edge on this one"

ASK snooker observers who would have been the most popular winner of a world title at the Crucible that never quite made it, and the chances are most will answer 'Jimmy White'. But a Welsh player from Carmarthen might not be too far behind the Whirlwind in that list. From the moment Matthew Stevens made his debut at the World Championship, he just looked completely at home in the arena, and his abilities shone brighter in Sheffield than anywhere else on the circuit.

Stevens had a fluency, technique and temperament that just seemed made to withstand the peculiar rigours and pressures generated by the intimate auditorium, and with the exception of a Masters title in 2000 as a very young professional, almost all his greatest days came at the Crucible.

After qualifying for his debut at the World Championship in 1998, Stevens cast aside any notion that he would be content with appearing on that stage, and reached the quarter-finals, beating Canada's Alain Robidoux and Essex's Mark King, only losing 13-10 to defending champion Ken Doherty.

In one six-year period from 2000 to 2005, Stevens appeared in the semi-finals no fewer than five times, going on to play in the final twice. The first of those occasions was against compatriot Mark Williams in 2000, a contest in which Stevens led 13-7 at one point. He was to lose 11 of the next 14 frames, but even this damaging loss did not overly dent the bravado of youth. Stevens was sure there would be other chances, and he was not wrong in that assumption.

Stevens says: "I loved playing at the Crucible, I had played well there and I think my record in Sheffield over the years proved that.

"Going right back to my debut there, I got to the quarter-finals that year losing to Ken who was defending champion, and got to the final again that year – but I beat Alain Robidoux and Mark King to get there.

"I think I felt instantly at home in that arena. Those years in the late 90s and early 2000s I was playing well and filled with so much confidence I fancied myself anywhere, but I especially enjoyed the long matches at the Crucible in that auditorium.

"From that first year playing there in 1998, I really expected to win it over those next eight years or so, and obviously I got close. I got deep in the tournament a few times, I think it is six semi-finals altogether with two finals.

"There can't be too many players who haven't won it who have a better Crucible record than me, apart from Jimmy White.

"And I am fortunate, there are plenty of fans who seem to like the way I played the game, and also appreciated how much I loved the Crucible and came alive there. You build up a following, and I have always been pretty down to earth and shared my success and failure with those fans.

"I got to the quarters again in 1999, losing to Hendry, but even when I lost to Mark Williams in the final in 2000 without a doubt I was sure I would be back as champion and winning it one year. I think I was 22 that year, it is hard to believe how young I was. Not many players that young get to a world final, only Judd in recent years.

"You didn't appreciate it at the time, it is only afterwards in later life that you realise what you were doing. And I was only a couple of balls away against Mark in that 2000 final really, I was 13-7 up and close to being world champion.

"At 13-7 in the dressing room there was no doubt I was going to win the title. I missed a black into the middle cueing over the blue that should have seen me go 14-8, that was important.

"There were semi-finals in the next two years, against John [Higgins] in 2001 and then Peter Ebdon in 2002, that was another terrific match. In 2002 I beat John in the quarter-finals, and got a 145 in that match which proved to be the high break that year. Then I was a ball away from beating Peter in the semi-final.

"I have been involved in some great matches at the Crucible, and that 2002 semi-final against Peter for me personally might have been the best. I made a lot of good breaks, and played better than him throughout really but we all know what he is like – he never gave up."

There were semi-final defeats to John Higgins (17-15 in 2001), Peter Ebdon in a match that could quite conceivably have featured in this book in greater detail (17-16 in 2002), and Graeme Dott (17-15 in 2004).

When Stevens, still only 27, reached the final for the second time in 2005, despite the sensational form shown in that year's competition by opponent Shaun Murphy he was the favourite to finally lift the trophy. But with the scar count starting to build Stevens suffered a painful 18-16 defeat to Murphy, who at 22 became the second-youngest world champion after Stephen Hendry.

It was a phenomenal triumph for Murphy, who emerged from a strong family snooker background, and had therefore been on the radar for some years through his junior exploits, and for unusually being allowed to turn professional at just 15 in 1998.

Murphy perhaps had it easier than some on his way up, benefiting from sponsorship while living in Northamptonshire, and also the motivation of father Tony to provide him with opportunity and high-class practice partners.

Qualifying for the World Championships of 2002 and 2003 helped Murphy, whose progress had been largely unspectacular to that point, climb the rankings. But it was still from No.48, and odds of 150-1, that he claimed that famous success in 2005, just the third qualifier after Alex Higgins in 1972 and Terry Griffiths in 1979 to win the world title.

And what all this meant was that when Murphy and Stevens came through to face each other in the quarter-finals in 2007 for a place in the last four and the single-table set-up, just two years after that final, there was plenty riding on it.

Murphy had done in 2005 what Stevens had failed to do in his own career – seize the first realistic chance to come along to get a world title under his belt. In the years that followed, and there were many tough defeats for the Magician not least in semi-finals of ranking tournaments, it was something that could never be taken away from him.

Murphy says: "With the old ranking system if you were a Crucible specialist, as Matthew was, you could almost make or break your season based on how you did there and at the UK Championship.

"Matthew was a phenomenal player at the Crucible with a very strong record there, and since then I had the same manager as he had in Brandon Parker and learned more about how he tended to peak for the World Championship.

"He should have won the year against Mark Williams in the final, and should have beaten me from 10-6 up in the 2005 final. There was a frame towards the end of the third session where he played a shot on the blue left-handed, was that a turning point? There were ley moments in the match and I did feel like I fell over the line in that final.

"We actually hadn't played a proper match in between 2005 and 2007 at the Crucible, I think just one match in some kind of *Pot Black* single-frame revival.

"When Matt got to the final in 2000, he probably expected to win it in the future. When I won it in 2005, I expected to win it again in the next ten years and many other events on the back of it, but it doesn't always work like that. You are not entitled to anything in snooker, or sport, or life really."

For Stevens, realisation was dawning that talent and a liking for the Crucible Theatre venue alone was not going to win him the prize he craved above all others. It took a lot to rattle the generally placid Stevens, but the 2005 final loss to Murphy had cut him to the quick.

He adds: "I had another close semi-final defeat in 2004 losing 17-15 to Graeme Dott and then I got to my second final against Shaun in 2005.

"And I have to be honest; this one really did hurt, more than the 2000 final, and some of these other very close semi-finals. I didn't play that well throughout in 2005 or in the final itself, and when I did produce anything like my best, it was towards the end of the final.

"Shaun went for everything, and potted everything, as he had been throughout the tournament. He was the underdog and while I didn't expect to lose, he found this amazing form at just the right time.

"I remember sitting in my apartment after the semi-final wondering how on earth I was in the final, I hadn't played anywhere near how I had played in previous years when I had failed to reach the final. But maybe it was the experience, I was just getting through. It was a strange season.

"But losing the final did hurt. I was still only 27, well under 30, but this felt like one I should have won, the time and opportunity for me to get that world title. I had been a big favourite at the start of the final. But from 16-16 he has knocked in breaks of 97 and 83, and I hardly went for a ball.

"There was a black he got that left me thinking, 'A lot of players just wouldn't have gone for that, let alone got it.' He was fearless, no scars, and was getting everything."

Stevens was therefore supremely motivated to exercise a measure of revenge against Murphy in 2007. Life had also dealt him some unkind cards, though these were to Stevens' huge credit never used as excuses. Father, mentor, chauffeur, friend and biggest supporter Morrell died unexpectedly in 2001, following the Masters success.

And earlier in the 2006–07 season Stevens had seen his best friend Paul Hunter lose his battle with cancer at the tragically premature age of just 27. If the loss of Hunter was felt most keenly by his family, and then the game itself, the effect on Stevens was considerable. The pair, with totally different personalities, were inseparable on tour.

Stevens beat Joe Delaney easily in round one, before seeing off Crucible debutant Mark Allen to reach the last eight. Murphy, meanwhile, had warmed up for another clash with the Welshman with a win over a youthful Judd Trump (10-6), and then veteran John Parrott (13-8).

He says: "I had beaten Judd Trump in the first round, his debut I think. It got to 6-5 to him before I realised I could only beat him one way, keep leaving him tempting long low-percentage reds and hope he'd miss a few, and eventually that's the way it panned out, five frames in a row.

"Then it was John Parrott, and I won the last five frames of that one as well from 8-8. On paper I was a big favourite, but I had caught up in the nostalgia generated from his first-round match against Steve Davis, and there was a lot of joking with the crowd that I got caught up in until I was reminded by my camp at 8-8 that I could lose this."

Murphy snapped out of it just in time against the 1991 world champion Parrott, winning the last five frames – an ominous portent of what was to come in the quarter-final.

He did well to hold Stevens to 4-4 after the first session, despite breaks of 46, 118, 64, 43 and 108 from the Welshman. But in the second session Stevens cut loose to establish what looked certain to be a match-winning advantage of 11-5, requiring just two more for victory.

Stevens recounts: "When you are young you have no battle scars but you do pick up a few along the way, the damaging defeats, ones that really hurt, along with any misses or mistakes you may have had in those matches and you have to process them and deal with them.

"And of course with what had happened two years before at the Crucible there was a bit of edge on this one, definitely, it just made you that little bit more determined to win.

"So with these extra things riding on it, and bear in mind it was a huge game anyway in its own right, a World Championship quarter-final for a place in the semi-finals and another real chance to win the title, I was very up for the game.

"And yet again as so often at the Crucible, I played really well in the first two sessions, and particularly the night and second session.

"From 4-4 in the morning I have won that session 7-1 to go 11-5 up, and kept him away from the table for large spells. I think he got about five points in the last three frames of the evening, and when I watched the highlights later I was pleased with how I played.

"And again I took it for granted, at 11-5 I thought I was in the semis again for what would have been the sixth time, and a tie against either Mark Selby or Ali Carter who were still playing."

Murphy, not generally short on self-belief, had almost given up the ghost. Lunch arrangements were being made in the courtesy car on the way to the venue, and there was just a faint hope that Stevens might surrender another large lead before a chance sighting irrevocably altered Murphy's mindset walking out for the final morning session.

He recalls: "I always had a huge respect for Matt and awareness of how good he was. With the bookies I was probably just favourite, but I didn't feel favourite to beat him especially at the Crucible. I had looked up to him as a junior, because of how he played the game, he was a god at that level.

"And that uncertainty contributed to how I played at the start, too much respect for him maybe, and I found myself 11-5 down after the second session. The third session was in the morning, friends and family said to me 'We'll probably see you for a coffee in a little while,' because it is very unlikely you can win from 11-5 in the best-of-25. We were discussing where to go for lunch in the car.

"I had set myself the target of getting to the mid-session interval as a pride thing, for some scoreline respectability, and if you did that who knows. Matthew had lost matches from way ahead in his career and you know that, so you have to try and see what happens. He lost to Mark in the final in 2000, could have beaten Peter Ebdon in the 2002 semi-final…

"At 11-5 the tournament director knocks on my door ready to do the walk of death, you are a dead man walking in that situation. My dressing room was the further away, so I am walking down past Matthew's open dressing room door and saw some almost empty beer glasses, this being at 9.55am.

"Now I have no way of knowing if those drinks were Matthew's, they may well not have been, and probably weren't, they could have been from the night before, anything. There was nothing to show they were his. There were other people in there. But it didn't matter to me at that moment. In my head I was thinking and making a quite possibly wrong connection, 'Maybe they all think they have won, or he is very nervous.'

"Whatever the truth of it, it helped me at that moment, it changed my whole outlook walking out there. And I had gone from waiting for the last rites to be read, to wondering if maybe I could do this."

Resuming needing just two of a possible nine frames to get over the line, Stevens lost the first of the day, before squandering a chance to go 12-6 up in the next. He did find a break of 52 to make it 12-7 in frame 19, and at that time there was no doubt in his mind he would still win the match.

But then the Murphy comeback started in earnest, and Stevens describes very eloquently just what a horrible sensation it is to have an opponent coming back at you as the momentum swings in his direction.

He says: "After Shaun got the first of the morning I probably should have gone 12-6 up, six up with seven to play, and I definitely should have won 13-7, losing that frame on the colours that made it 12-8. And I remember him giving it the big fist at that moment as we went off for the mid-session interval.

"And I was asking myself, 'Why is he doing that, giving it the big fist…I am still 12-8 up and I am going to win? I can't lose this.' It did wind me up a little bit. And from that moment I crumbled a bit.

"I had a chance to win 13-10 but missed a black trying to get on the last red on the cushion, and then could have won 13-11 in the next but Shaun got in with a couple of reds left on the table. By the time it got to 12-12 I was struggling and after he made a 40-odd I never really had a chance.

"It was a tough one to swallow, a double whammy because not only did I really want to win after the 2005 final, but it cost me a place back in the top 16 and back then that was a lot more important, being there for the whole season. I think it was Ryan Day who needed Murphy to win to get into the 16, so he was happy at least.

"That is one of the matches in my career, and there have been a couple, where you really can't quite believe it got away. I think that was the worst, and the most disappointed I have ever been after a match. I hadn't played well during the season, but as so often had found something at the Crucible.

"And again I had a great chance to win the title, or at least give myself that chance, but I had come up short, plus not getting back in the 16. I blew it really, and you can probably hear just talking about it now nearly ten years later, it still hurts!

"It is a horrible feeling when someone is coming back at you when you had a big lead, the worst really. It is in your head, 'I should be back in my apartment now,' and it is hard to explain how it can mess with your head. A bit like you are drunk, just reeling.

"And if it has happened to you before in a big match, of course it is there if you are in a similar situation again. It does now if it happens to me. But people remember those, and forget all the ones you won from ahead and behind.

"Look at Jimmy, he is known for losing six finals, but he won more matches at the Crucible than most, and I haven't done too badly, I am above a good few champions in the list of matches won there and that is something to be proud of looking back."

At the end Murphy could not quite believe what he had done, but was sure some tactics in the arena adopted to try and cope with the unbearable tension in the decider once he had got back from 12-7 to 12-12 helped make the difference.

He says: "As I began to claw my way back, I had some friends in London in the audience sat four or five rows back. And Matthew kept leaving the arena, it was obvious he was starting to feel uncomfortable in that bear-pit it can be at the Crucible.

"But with less to lose I stayed out there between frames and embraced it. At 12-12 he went out for what seemed an eternity, and the other match had finished by this time. I stood in the middle of the arena practising my golf swing with my cue extension. I think it helped me acclimatise to the tension, and made it more bearable in that decider."

Chapter 16

Steve Davis v John Higgins, 2010, last 16

"I walked through a packed Tudor Square and a corridor of cheering people up to the Winter Garden afterwards, it was like a golfer going up the 18th after winning a title"

THE 2010 World Championship is one that will linger in the memory for many reasons, not all of them positive, and those aspects we will return to later.

But the exhilarating high-point, even if eventual winner Neil Robertson might well disagree, was a last-16 contest between the defending champion and a 52-year-old chasing one last hurrah at a venue he had graced for more than 30 years.

Before however we focus again on Steve Davis, already featured extensively in these pages, let us have a detailed look at both John Higgins, and also the backdrop to the tournament with snooker undergoing a period of turbulent change in the governance of the sport.

Scotland's Higgins had been one of the 'golden crop' turning professional in 1992 along with Ronnie O'Sullivan and Mark Williams. At the time of writing the trio have amassed a total of 74 ranking titles and 11 Masters titles between them with the prospect of more to come, and within those ranking-event successes 11 world titles.

From Glasgow, swiftly dubbed 'The Wizard of Wishaw' and backed by a strong family unit, Higgins served early notice of his ability and talent by winning a first ranking title at just 19 – the Skoda Grand Prix at the Assembly Rooms in Derby, with a 9-6 win over Dave Harold.

Benefiting from a ready supply of high-quality practice partners north of the border, Higgins was regularly in the business end of the major tournaments, winning about as many finals as he lost until 1998 from when he won seven showpieces in a row over three years, including a first World Championship final in 1998 when he beat Ken Doherty 18-12.

Higgins was and remains a master tactician, a magnificent break-builder and possessed of a cussed streak that was invaluable in a matchplay situation, being both able to bully opponents when in front, and have them sweating when he came back at them from behind. And all of these attributes swiftly singled him out as the heir apparent to Stephen Hendry in Scotland.

Higgins and long-time English rival O'Sullivan seemed to spur each other on, and so it was no surprise that after the Rocket won a second world title in 2004, Higgins did the same in 2007, with the dynamic duo then picking up another one apiece in the next two years.

Now 34, Higgins as the 2009 winner therefore arrived in Sheffield playing first up on the Saturday morning against Barry Hawkins, and to a finish in the second session in the evening. No player since Hendry in 1996 had defended the world title, something of which Higgins was only too aware given his roots.

Speaking to journalist Neil Goulding in the *Daily Record* in April that year, Higgins said: "It's going to be so tough but I feel I've got every chance. I managed to hold my nerve last season and that was one of the big things I took from the tournament because as you get older you start to feel the pressure more.

"It was great to keep myself under control and that can be the fine line between winning and losing. It's been a good season but that will all count for nothing if I have a bad World Championship. Although I've got to No.1 now, I haven't thought about that much because my focus is on trying to defend the title. It would be amazing to be world champion and No.1 at the same time – that's what I'm aiming for."

The 'good season' Higgins referred to was one in which the players had only been provided with five ranking tournaments before the World Championship, so the Scot winning one of them – the Welsh Open – and getting to the final of another at the UK Championship, was commendable.

And it was this dearth of events as much as anything that had seen the previous chairman of the WPBSA Sir Rodney Walker lose a vote of confidence in December 2009, paving the way for promoter Barry Hearn to take control – first of the WPBSA, and then later World Snooker and the commercial rights through a close vote later in the summer of 2010. Higgins had been one of the fiercest critics of the former regime, over what he saw as an inability to take the game to new markets.

Other turmoil to throw into the mix ahead of this particular World Championship was the travel chaos caused by the Icelandic volcano ash cloud, seeing referees fail to arrive from mainland Europe, and Mark Allen grab the last possible ferry from Northern Ireland to make his first-day 10am start, arriving at midnight the day before. It was all a prelude to eruptions of a very different kind later in the tournament.

So back to Davis, then. Though a six-time world champion and arguably its greatest ever ambassador, the Nugget's time as a competitor at the top level looked just about over. By his own admission he was delighted to qualify for the World Championship, had not won a match at the Crucible for four years, and apart from the win over Adrian Gunnell to get him to Sheffield had only won one ranking-event match all season, a qualifier in the UK Championship.

This was the twilight of Davis's career, his reputation transformed from ruthless winner to much-loved and feted national treasure, and playing for love with little expectation. His last major title had come in 1997, mounting a Masters final comeback against Ronnie O'Sullivan, and there had been a glorious run to the final of the 2005 UK Championship before losing to Ding Junhui.

But while Davis prepared for a match against Mark King, Higgins had to play Hawkins, a player at that time lacking confidence when up against the very best. Higgins failed to hit top gear, but as expected won through with a 10-6 scoreline.

He said: "I was a total bag of nerves early on. I knew it was going to happen because that's how I felt on the two previous occasions I've come back here as the champion."

But Higgins was also convinced that he would be more relaxed against either King, the favourite to emerge from the first-round match starting on the Monday night, or Davis in the last 16.

Incredibly, though, Davis found some technical tinkering used during his qualifying win stood up to the sterner test against King as he edged through 10-9 – knowing he would now face Higgins.

In his post-match press conference after the win over King, Davis looked a like a kid in a sweetshop with a golden ticket stuffed in his back pocket for good measure, and simply couldn't stop smiling.

He said: "I think I've got some dog in the next round…who is it again? I haven't been looking much further than my qualifiers recently, let alone the first round.

"But to play John Higgins here, the world champion, I am just going to love it and it's great. Hopefully I will raise my standard and it can happen against a great player that you have nothing to lose.

"I will try to win it, I'm fed up with making up the numbers. I actually feel as if I am playing all right, but it is going to be tough, he is hard. Three sessions of granite, that is what I need – that and a Zimmer frame."

Reflecting back, he says: "There were a couple of years when I didn't qualify, and then a run when I did – but I had lost in the first round for the previous three years at the Crucible.

"I was starting to lose touch with the sharp end of the game, though I still had moments and experiences when I competed properly. I had never stopped, even at the age of 52 or whatever I was then, working on my technique.

"I would go off with my father and we prepared like that on the practice table, trying to get everything right.

"He would try and spot certain things and tell me what to do, others I would do myself. And that year I decided I wasn't staying down long enough on the shot, and hitting the ball positively enough.

"And in the qualifiers that year I was more deliberate and not getting up quickly and it was working, as I beat Adrian Gunnell to make it through. He was so upset, distraught! I'm not sure he ever fully recovered from that, falling off the tour not long afterwards.

"Then at the Crucible I had Mark King in the first round and I knew he would be a handful, a hard, clever player and a typical first-round panic match.

"I scrambled through, falling over the line really – and my reward was a match against John Higgins at the Crucible. And that was just incredible for me, an occasion to really savour at that stage of my life and career."

And so the scene and stage were set for a meeting of arguably the strongest player in the world at the time, or at least vying with O'Sullivan for that billing, and the ageing champion hauling himself back into the ring for one last shot at glory. What happened next was little short of miraculous.

No one, including Davis himself, thought he had a chance against Higgins. The Scot was occasionally prone to lapses in form and could beat himself up over those with the best of them, but surely his worst Z-game would still be too good for his opponent this time?

King gave Higgins a hint of the no-win situation and pressure he might face, and what he could expect from the Crucible crowd, in his own post-match press conference following the first round.

He had said: "I have never had a crowd that against me ever, which is understandable, and I did let it get to me at times. I had a few texts from other players when I got Steve in the draw saying it wasn't worth him turning up, but that annoyed me. Not in a million years would I think Steve was an easy draw whether he was 52 or 72, he is a class act."

By any reading of the match Davis needed a good start to stand the remotest chance, even if it was to avoid an embarrassing drubbing – and that is just what he got, winning the last four frames of the first session with breaks of 72, 102 and 63 to move 6-2 ahead on the first day of the three.

And though Higgins, who had started the match a 1-16 favourite with the bookmakers, came to the party in the second session, mustering breaks of 78 and 106, Davis was just about keeping him at bay – crucially coming up with a break of 55 in frame 16 to lead 9-7 overnight going in to the climax on Saturday afternoon.

Davis says: "I can honestly say in my heart of hearts I never for one moment seriously believed that I could beat him in that match. The one big advantage I had was that I had absolutely nothing to lose against John, it is a far easier scenario than many I faced in my career.

"I suppose if you got absolutely humiliated on your favourite stage and ended up wondering what you were doing there, that was the worst that could have happened to me.

"But basically I had a free shot at it, and something to really enjoy. I felt that I was having some success with my new technical changes, and I knew what shots to play.

"I knew exactly how good a matchplayer John was, and though this might sound strange from someone who had won it six times, at this moment it was an honour to play him.

"And I just played great. I couldn't have asked for a better start than I got, he didn't play well and I came off after the first session leading 6-2 with everyone thinking 'I didn't see that one coming', including me.

"Of course you try and put yourself in John's mind and he knows if he loses it is a massive story and shock. But the thing about session matches is that at 6-2 now I do have something to lose. He came back at me but I was still 9-7 up and I could live with that, it was damage limitation and winning the last of the second session to be two ahead was huge."

Higgins quickly levelled at 9-9 with breaks of 70 and 115, but Davis's experience screamed at him that he was actually still playing to a high standard and still in the contest, not least because of the huge pressure on his opponent.

Davis recalls: "John came out and made a couple of big breaks and it seemed like it might be business as usual. And from there it is an easy one to play for me, win or lose. There is no embarrassment if I lose, no regret, no could have or should have, it is just a fair fight.

"He kept coming back as he does, to 11-11 after I led again and then somehow I managed to see it out. I was playing decent, cueing okay, and not slipping into bad habits. I relished the challenge."

The last frame was for drama in its own way the equal of the one Davis lost to Dennis Taylor in the final all those years before. Well as Davis had played, Higgins had not been at his best and all the frustrations experienced by the Scot were neatly encapsulated in the thrilling denouement.

Higgins, fighting as he had been all match to stay alive, was in first with 42 but miscalculated going in to the pack off a black and finished on nothing. He then had another good chance, but could not make more than one after catching a red on the baulk cushion full ball with his positional shot, as sagely predicted moments before by Ken Doherty on BBC commentary.

But left another easy red to the middle pocket Higgins contrived the miss of the match, allowing Davis to get back into it with a run of 33. And when Higgins blinked first in a safety exchange on the yellow, Davis cleared up to the pink helped by a brilliant double on the final brown with which he also managed to knock the blue on the cushion over a pocket.

As the pink went in the crowd erupted very much in the style of that Icelandic volcano, a magnanimous if devastated Higgins came over with a genuine handshake and words of congratulation, and a disbelieving Davis held his head with his hand while taking the acclaim – the oldest man into the quarter-finals for 27 years.

In his post-match press conference, a stunned Higgins said of his boyhood hero: "You know Steve is capable of putting pressure on you but you think as he is getting older he is not going to be able to produce the standard of even the last seven years when he has played some great matches. It is fantastic, really.

"The red to the middle in the last frame was a bad shot, a very bad shot. My cueing was not good, I was snatching at everything and at the end I knew Steve was going to clear up. The balls never, ever forgive you in this game.

"I missed some crucial pots in the match. Last year I managed to hold myself together under the pressure, this year I was all over the place. It may be unlike me, but it happens, and it was tough.

"I felt fine going into the final session, but I knew I had been struggling. I was trying to scrap it out with Steve because he was by far the better player in my eyes. His cue ball control was a lesson to me, I was running out of position so many times. But if I wasn't at my best, I certainly wasn't at my worst and Steve played great snooker.

"All his career he has had great cue ball control, that's part of what has made him such a great player. It was just a lesson. It may be a fairytale, but it is at my expense. He is 52, and last year I was 33 and I was dead on my feet after some monumental clashes but he's probably fitter than me. He was a big underdog against me but has been out there more than most and knew how to handle it.

"Childhood idol? No, no – I hated him out there! I was looking at him despising him and wishing he would collapse or something! But seriously, when the match ball is done, it's done, you wish him all the best and that's what you have to do."

Higgins actually did a fair bit better than wish Davis all the best, but at the time the six-time world champion was still coming to terms with how he had got over the winning line, before experiencing one of the best moments of his snooker life walking through a cheering Tudor Square up to the BBC studio in the Winter Garden. Even there the drama continued, with a 'Fathers for Justice' protester interrupting proceedings.

Davis recalls: "When it came to the colours I thought I might as well be aggressive, I wasn't going to tip-tap around. I played a very aggressive shot to play position for a double on the brown and knock the blue into a better position. It couldn't have gone better.

"All of a sudden I have to get the extension on my cue out to cut the blue in, and leave myself a pink into the middle, I was plum on it but shaking like a leaf. I was praying 'Please don't miss this.' All the effort just for this one shot. Towards the back end of my career I had developed what could be called a slice for a golfer, sending the cue ball off to the right, meaning I could miss to the left.

"Under severe pressure it got worse and was debilitating, so I was terrified that might happen but luckily it didn't. I told myself keep your head down and your cue down.

"It felt great to go out and win it in that fashion, and then afterwards I couldn't believe I had done it. I walked round to John and he said something like 'you're still the greatest', which was very classy.

"As I left the Crucible, I had to walk up to the studio where I was more used to working at that age. It had obviously been a sunny day with a lot of people outside in the square drinking and watching on the screens. And it felt like it had sucked people in, in the same way as me and Dennis all those years before.

"And that walk up was like walking through a corridor of people, maybe a bit like a golfer going up the 18th after winning a title but they were all much closer. The cheers were amazing, it was like a fairytale. Then I had to sit in the studio where I was used to being a professional in a different way.

"It was a great feeling – but then the protester came along and we had the security springing into life. It was over quickly and Hazel is such a pro, she coped admirably."

The frenzy of interest in the result was phenomenal, and I can honestly confirm one of the two or three busiest days I have spent as a journalist at the Crucible. Davis's formal retirement in 2016 was one of the others, proving the sporting nostalgia market continues to thrive.

Phil Yates, in *The Observer* the next day, immediately offered the comparison with another grizzled sporting great. He wrote: "The Tom Watson feelgood factor has been recreated at the Crucible by Steve Davis who, at 52, defied snooker logic to become the oldest quarter-finalist for 27 years in the World Championship. Last July at Turnberry, Watson, 59, put Tiger Woods and Co in the shade before cruelly losing out on the Claret Jug in a play-off with Stewart Cink. Davis, equally determined to strike a blow for sport's elder statesmen, beat John Higgins, the defending champion, 13-11."

Davis could not do it again against Robertson in the quarter-finals going down 13-5, and the win over Higgins was to prove his last at the Crucible, the first having come in 1980 against Patsy Fagan.

But for Higgins, bad was about to become much worse. The 1998 film *Sliding Doors* carries as its main plot premise the idea that one moment can irrevocably alter a life's course. And the unexpected defeat to Davis triggered a chain of events that saw Higgins fly out to Kiev with his former manager Pat Mooney rather than preparing for a quarter-final in Sheffield, in theory to discuss backing for a World Series of Snooker they were launching.

Instead Higgins and Mooney were filmed by undercover reporters in a sting operation for the first discredited and now defunct *News of the World*, a video the newspaper claimed appeared to show the pair discussing the possibility of losing frames for money.

The story was published on the first day of the final between Robertson and Graeme Dott, and as well as altering Higgins' life almost totally overshadowed that showpiece. Higgins swiftly issued a statement denying any wrongdoing, insisting that he never had and never would fix a frame or match for money, vowing to clear his name.

And an independent tribunal chaired by Ian Mill QC in September saw two charges of match-fixing and corruption dropped, leaving Higgins cleared of all of the most serious allegations. Mill accepted Higgins' assertions that he did not know anything in advance about what was going to be discussed, and also that anything he said was in fear of his safety and desire to leave as quickly as possible.

However, Higgins was banned from snooker for six months and fined £75,000 after being found guilty of the lesser charges of failing to report an approach, and giving the impression to the undercover reporters that he might break the betting rules.

Once Higgins had left Sheffield and remembering the tribunal was some months away from being played out, it was left to those high-profile snooker figures still at the Crucible, including Davis, to cope with the barrage of media questions. And this was not easy for any concerned, since at that time no one had any definitive answers.

The furore could have made Hearn step away or think again – instead he took the story as a cue to tighten betting rules and make as part of his pitch for the right to run the game the need for snooker to be seen as whiter than white.

Hearn says: "It is obviously very strange looking back at the match retrospectively, given what happened later to John Higgins. I thought all that did take a little bit of the shine off Steve's achievement. But on the day none of that applied anyway because it was all still to come. On the day, it was incredible.

"It was up there with his win over Ronnie O'Sullivan in the Masters final in 1997 for me, as the two greatest wins of his later career. Higgins was the modern-day master cueman and that win probably extended Steve's playing career by a few years, with the boost and belief it gave him.

"He might have retired had he lost in the first round that year but was really proud of himself over beating Higgins, a mature pride, not like in 1981. He was leading his army for one last hurrah, and what a hurrah – centre stage at the Crucible.

"It is a justification of how you have spent your life. You know Father Time keeps coming, King Canute couldn't send the waves back and neither can you as a sportsman, but there are moments when you feel in there and still capable."

The only disappointment for Davis was that within days of one of the most satisfying results of his career he had to answer questions of a very different sort as one of the figureheads of the game.

He says: "I wish what happened afterwards had not have happened for all sorts of reasons. Of course from John's perspective it wouldn't have been a good year after that match, though the more serious charges as we know were dropped, leaving him clear of those. Had he beaten me, he would almost certainly never have gone to Kiev.

"For me it went from having one of the most amazing moments and World Championships of my life, and all that euphoria and excitement, to having to answer a very different set of questions.

"And that was tough. None of us knew the full story, just what had been reported, but as high-profile figures we were being asked to react."

None of that, though, could in truth take away from one of Davis's best ever wins, a glorious last Crucible victory that earned him unprecedented standing ovations in every session – and unlike so many in his 1980s pomp, one that no one expected him to pull off.

Chapter 17

Neil Robertson v Martin Gould, 2010, last 16

"Going for a practice before the last session I became really worried – it felt like someone had chopped my arm off, I couldn't hit a ball properly and I was thinking, 'God, not today, not this'"

WHENEVER Neil Robertson reflects on his first World Championship win at the Crucible, achieved with an 18-13 success over Graeme Dott in the final, it will be with a sharp intake of breath as he recalls how his title charge was so nearly quashed before it had really got going.

In most sporting success stories there are fateful moments that with hindsight appear laden with extra meaning and significance, and the Australian's last-16 encounter with the hitherto little-known Martin Gould fits neatly into that category.

Robertson was to execute an act of escapology that would have brought a smile to the face of Harry Houdini himself, extricating himself from an abyss created by Gould with two scintillating sessions of play, only for the occasion to creep up on the Londoner with the winning line in sight.

But that was not before the Crucible crowd and millions of television viewers had been treated to a stunning exhibition from Gould that left Robertson wondering out loud at one stage if "he has borrowed the soul of Ronnie O'Sullivan".

By 2010 the left-handed Robertson was one of the best players in the world. He had famously arrived back in the UK in 2003 for a third crack at the professional tour after two failed attempts, with £500 in his pocket and little else in the way of baggage and belongings.

But this time, basing himself in Cambridge and with the mentoring help of Joe Perry, Robertson was ready. Some of the comments from opponents during his first two sorties into the pro game still rankled, that he had been in some way a 'good draw'.

And Robertson came back a different and determined animal, taking advice wherever it was offered from players he respected, notably on how to improve his safety game and positional play, and this all added to a temperament that looked made for the peculiar mental demands of snooker.

Robertson, an engaging character and a fine ambassador for his sport, had won all four of the ranking event finals he had contested to that point, showing he was more than happy on that stage, and earlier this season had won the Grand Prix in Glasgow.

So he was a big favourite against qualifier Gould, 28, who was appearing at the World Championship for only a second time, having lost to Mark Allen in the first round the previous year.

Gould was a tidy, compact player with a smooth cue action and as he was later to relate, had almost stumbled across a more forceful and attacking style of play that appeared to suit him in the weeks leading up to his first-round match against Hong Kong's Marco Fu.

The Pinner player had left the tour some years previously at a time when much of his time and energies had been devoted to caring for his mother Shirley, suffering from cancer, and who he was to lose to the disease in 2004. But Gould, after hardly playing for almost four years, was back on the circuit in 2007 having won a second English Amateur Championship, on a re-spotted black in the decider, and then the English play-offs.

Gould had been a part-time croupier at one time at a casino in north London, a nugget that was to surface and resurface during his excursion into the World Championship limelight along with a variety of substandard puns from an all-too-predictable media pack.

And to set up the match with Robertson he had already had to beat Belgium's Bjorn Haneveer and former Crucible finalist Nigel Bond in the qualifying rounds, and then Fu 10-9 in a thriller that saw Gould make a cool 90 in the decisive final frame.

Gould says: "The season had been an absolute nightmare, and I had to play a couple of qualifiers to get to the Crucible. I had taken a couple of hammerings along the way, as well.

"I think maybe I won one match, and then not another one until the World qualifiers. I had to play Bjorn Haneveer and had I lost I'd have been out of the top 48, so a lot of pressure when you haven't won for a long time.

"I got jittery near the winning line but fell over it and something just seemed to change in me and it released my natural style and opened the floodgates.

"Next it was Nigel Bond, a former finalist, for a place at the World Championship and everything I took on seemed to fly in.

"I had gone from being really negative and fearful and become this really attacking player, an approach I also had taken in a recent mixed pairs match with Pam Wood.

"My game had gone full circle but I took this different style and a little bit of confidence into the qualifiers, and then the first match against Marco Fu. If it was working, why change it?

"I don't think I had gone totally reckless, but it worked for me. I always seemed to fall behind at the Crucible, and again I was 4-1 down to Marco. But I hung in there, made some good breaks in the second session and then a 90 in the decider for a 10-9 win that was really big for me against such a good player on this stage.

"I had a few days off before the next one and hung around Sheffield – but really I didn't know what to expect. I was into uncharted territory against Neil, I had never played a match that long over the best-of-25 frames.

"I enjoy playing in front of the big crowds on the big stage, though that hadn't happened too much up to that point.

"Most players thrive in front of a crowd of 1,000 or more; playing in empty arenas is tough if you like to perform but you don't always get the opportunity and have to adapt and cope.

"Here I was in the last 16 at the Crucible, which was great, but at that time the off-table attention was new. I am usually quite a quiet and private person.

"I told myself that even against Neil if I played the way I had been, I could win – but mainly to try and enjoy the occasion. That is especially important at the Crucible, because it can eat you alive if you are not enjoying it."

However ,when the match began, events soon took an unexpected turn. Robertson scored just 26 points in the first four frames as he fell 4-0 behind, and further breaks of 43 and 53 from Gould put him 6-0 ahead in this best-of-25-frame encounter.

Robertson recalls: "I knew a bit about Martin and that he was a dangerous player, but I had never seen him play like that before, and certainly hadn't been expecting him to play like that. And especially given the circumstances, the stage and the setting – it is such a big tournament and he was playing in the longest match of his life to that point.

"Martin was running out of position on the black and then just knocking in long yellows, greens and blues, playing these absurd recovery shots, and there just wasn't anything I could do. I felt totally helpless.

"If that had been Ronnie O'Sullivan playing like he did against me for two sessions, everyone in the media would have been hailing him as a genius.

"Martin just played out of his skin, and it really was a case of, 'Where did that come from?'

"Nobody can compete if your opponent just doesn't miss anything, and when I was sitting there 6-0 down in that first session it was just incredible.

"To be honest I was absolutely delighted to win the last two frames of the session and trail only 6-2 going in to the second session. We played Friday morning, Friday night and then Saturday afternoon.

"And going in to the second session the one thing cheering me up was that I thought, 'There is absolutely no way he can play like that again.' But he did!

"He just kept going for the same balls, and kept getting them. He was putting me under all sorts of pressure and I just didn't have the answers. If I was being ultra-harsh about my own game, maybe my safety wasn't quite as good as it might have been, not perfect. But he was punishing even really good safeties.

"And again, I pulled off a near-miracle to only lose the session 5-3 and be 11-5 down, it could have been all over that night, easily."

Understandably, Gould was enjoying himself. He remembers: "The first six frames I don't think I missed a pot, or anything. I looked at Neil in his chair and he had an expression that seemed to say, 'Where has this come from – who are you?' And to be fair, he wasn't the only one.

"You know you have something in the locker, you just need it to come out at the right time and it did at the start of that match, at the biggest tournament, with millions watching.

"Of course I was disappointed ultimately not to see it out – I just wish I could have finished the match on Friday night. But the night to sleep on it was to do me no favours, I was thinking too much about it.

"The last break of 63 I made on the Friday was crazy, I had made two stupid plants, swerved round reds to pot a green, and I so wanted to carry on, but it had to stop."

After two sessions of the match Gould led 11-5, and if anything his opponent Robertson was equally delighted with the scoreline, having been battered like a ship in a storm for most of the 16 frames played.

There were glimmers of hope in the deep recesses of Robertson's mind, but not enough to stop him checking out of his apartment that Saturday morning ahead of the third and final afternoon session. But he might have felt a good deal more confident of a comeback had he known how Gould was feeling in his final practice on Saturday lunchtime.

Gould recalls: "I wish for that match only I had had someone in my corner, as I do now, to just calm me down and give the odd bit of advice. I had good friends, but they didn't really know what to say like a Terry Griffiths or a Steve Feeney.

"I distinctly remember going in for a final practice session on the Saturday lunchtime leading 11-5 and being really worried. It felt like someone had taken my arm away, I couldn't hit a ball properly and I was thinking, 'God, not today, not this.'

"From the moment I woke up it just felt like my arm had been chopped off and someone was telling me, 'You can't win today.' Whether that is pressure, I don't know. I had slept well."

Gould's gloomy premonitions proved to be well-founded, as his level dipped, and Robertson grew stronger.

He remembers: "I missed a black off the spot in the first frame of the afternoon. And then in the fifth frame of the afternoon with the score at 11-9 I got in again after I potted a pink, though the referee Olivier Marteel wasn't paying attention properly.

"I think he had been keeping an eye on someone in the crowd telling them to keep quiet, and that meant instead of picking the pink out of the pocket, he first took the white off the table for no reason.

"I saw it was about to happen, but I couldn't stop him. It really threw me because it was the first time I felt I had 'got in' in the final session. It took about three minutes to sort it out and replace the two balls, your rhythm goes, and I took on a tough red to the middle and missed it.

"Next thing I know it is 11-10, and at that stage I didn't think I could win a frame. It felt like everything had gone, and the pockets had got smaller.

"Somehow I got to 12-10, and was telling myself, 'Look, you've still got three chances to finish this.' But I didn't really get a chance until 12-12 when I started to feel good again.

"I made 40 and thought the red I took on the green pocket was in, but it caught the near jaw, it would have been all over – and I never got another look-in after he got a snooker. That was it, goodnight Vienna.

"The Steve Davis and John Higgins match, giving the winner of our match their next opponent, was finishing before ours started and I had told my friends not to let me know the result. As it turned out, that was virtually impossible.

"As I was being introduced into the arena though MC Rob Walker mentioned to the crowd about the famous shock victory we had seen earlier!

"The fact is we knew we were not just playing for a quarter-final place, but for a tie against a 52-year-old Steve Davis for a place in the semi-finals. I would rather not have known.

"I think Manchester United were playing Spurs, my team, that lunchtime and I didn't want to know that result either but one of the security guards told me we were losing 3-1! It just didn't feel like my day."

The Davis/Higgins match had provided an intriguing sub-plot to this contest. The winner was expecting to face Higgins for a place in the semi-finals. But all did not go to plan in the defending champion's last-16 tie with a now 52-year-old Davis.

And by the time Robertson began his fightback Davis had pulled off a huge shock, and looked a more comfortable draw on paper than Higgins for a place in the last four. Robertson had immediately seen the potential for this to adversely affect Gould.

Robertson adds: "I knew that Shaun Murphy had come back from way down a couple of years before against Matthew Stevens in a best-of-25 match, so that is in the back of your mind.

"But really Martin's level had to drop even if I played really well, if he carried on like that it was over – but luckily for me it did drop a little.

"I was asked if I wanted to renew the apartment for another week on Saturday morning and I said don't bother, I'm 11-5 down, and don't worry about it and let it out – I just asked if I could leave my stuff downstairs for one more day.

"We knew that the winner of our match would play Steve Davis or John Higgins, and obviously it was a huge shock him eventually beating John on the same day. I had been watching the final session on TV in the morning.

"We would have expected to be facing Higgins in the quarter-finals, but in their match that finished in the early afternoon on the Saturday it was Steve Davis, a legend in the sport but no longer at the peak of his powers, that had won.

"I think John just got sucked in to the challenge of taking on Steve at the tactical game rather than outscoring him, and it backfired badly.

"And I just really hoped that Martin was watching it, because for all Steve's status to play him for a place in the semi-finals was a real opportunity at that time. And the way Martin had played, he would have beaten Steve if he played in the same way.

"But these things can just add a little extra pressure, maybe get in to his head. Steve won, and we knew our opponent for the quarters. It didn't affect me at all, because I was in all sorts of trouble just trying to get back in the match.

"I resolved just to put him under as much pressure as possible, and I won the first two frames comfortably.

"And it was clear that Martin wasn't playing with quite the same freedom, or going for the same shots. He was feeling it. The ones he was going for weren't going in and he was missing them by quite some distance.

"I won the first five to get to 11-10 and should have gone 11-11, but missed the last red and he got to 12-10. From there I got it back to 12-12, he was in first with a 40 before rattling a red.

"I got a good long red under real pressure and made 52 off it, and put him in trouble on the last red before clearing up to the blue."

The victory left Robertson feeling almost invincible, and he knew enough about the psychology of this most mentally demanding of sports to recognise there could be spin-off benefits for him not just from the confidence it brought him, but the doubt it could instil in the minds of opponents.

"The win gave me a huge boost of confidence," he recalls. "You think that if you can come back from 11-5 down in a best-of-25, you can come back from almost any deficit. And it stood me in great stead for the rest of the World Championship.

"That sort of win sends out a clear message to your rivals that you can deal with adversity, and they knew I could come back. You see it with Mark Selby and John Higgins, the opponent knows they can come back and it adds pressure. The feeling is incredible winning a match like that at the Crucible. I actually kept my emotions pretty much in check for that one, which is not always the case with the fist-pumps and so on. I was calm and focused.

"And I was very conscious for that one of how Martin must be feeling. He had contributed hugely to a great match, and out of respect I waited until he had left the arena until I really let rip.

"Going forward I then knew I had to avoid any mistakes John Higgins had made against Steve, and if anything I over-attacked in that match, but luckily most of them went in. I knew there would be some value in winning easily and getting some extra rest.

"I was actually 12-2 up in the quarter-final and annoyed with myself for missing the chance to win with a session to spare as Steve won the last two of that second session.

"But I went on to beat Steve comfortably, and then played one of my best ever matches against Ali Carter in the semi-finals – that was almost a perfect performance. It was a great year for me, and obviously my world title would not have happened had I not dug so deep against Martin.

"I know he has said it didn't affect him too badly, but I do think it had a slight longer-term effect on him because he struggled for a while after that, so I was very pleased to see him win that ranking title in Berlin a few years later."

If Gould is not convinced as to exactly how many scars this defeat left, he was correctly happy to draw positives from an experience that had showed him capable of playing a level and style of snooker that brought him many new admirers.

He concludes: "I personally don't think it took me too long to get over it, but who knows. I did get very drunk that night with mates who had come up to Sheffield.

"And I stayed in the city for a few days, trying not to spend hours on my own over-thinking it. So I enjoyed my run despite the defeat.

"Sometimes it just isn't meant to be. In later years it didn't stop me winning my first ranking title in Germany, I kept getting mentioned in the list of best players not to have won one, and I had enough of it and resolved to get myself off that list that week in Berlin.

"But overall Barry Hearn coming in to run the game was good for me, the ranking system benefited me as did playing more, and I have shown resilience after bad defeats not only against Neil but in others during my career."

Chapter 18

Ding Junhui v Judd Trump, 2011, semi-final

"Ding and I are often thought of together for our ability and being close in age, and I have always thought of it as a bit of a grudge game – with him breaking through quicker than I did"

WHEN the two best young players from England and China respectively met on the single-table set-up at the Crucible chasing a place in the final of the 2011 World Championship, it was a match and a setting this particular correspondent had been keenly anticipating for years.

Incredibly despite the fact that Trump, still only 21, had been a professional for six years and Ding, 24, for eight this was only the second time they had met, and the first occasion since 2005, when China's No.1 had prevailed 9-2 in a UK Championship qualifier.

And the main reason for that was because the Bristol-born Trump had struggled to get to grips with the reduced circumstances of attempting to reach the venues for the major tournaments. He was a player that craved the big stages and crowds, but was playing most of the time in cubicles in front of the proverbial one man and his dog.

Then when he did get through, the pressure to do well and pick up points to get out of this living hell was so overwhelming that he often failed to deliver, and the cycle continued. The suspicion lingered, though, that inside lurked a talent that could not be shackled forever. It had to come out, for a player that had always used Ding as a marker – notably in an interview I did with him for the *Daily Express* in 2006.

In it Trump, who first made waves becoming the youngest player to make a 147 in competition aged 14, said: "I have seen what Ding has done. He is a very good player and has done really well, and I know people will make comparisons because of my age.

"If I could do what he has done in the last couple of years, I would be very happy. It can take time, and won't happen overnight. You can see that by the trouble he has had getting to the latter stages of events, which shows how tough it is in qualifiers."

But highly significantly, Trump had made his big breakthrough just two weeks before the World Championship by coming through as a qualifier to win the China Open in Beijing, for a first ranking title success.

Trump says: "In China I finally started to play okay at a big, ranking-event venue and it was such a relief really. Until then I had struggled to get out of qualifying and then when I did felt under huge pressure to make it count and wasn't doing myself justice.

"So to play so well in China and beat good players relatively comfortably in most cases up until the final was a huge boost to my confidence and really kick-started things in my career.

"Then the final itself was a good one against Mark Selby, and the whole thing just took a lot of pressure off going in to the World Championship. I had my title, I knew I could build on it, and I had almost a free shot at Neil Robertson, the defending champion, in the first round."

Ding, like Trump hailed as a child prodigy from his early teens, experienced some similar distaste for the less glamorous qualifying stages when he first joined the tour, but like Trump and others over the years was simply too good not to ultimately escape the treadmill and start winning titles.

His father, a maker of teapots in Jiangsu Province in China, encouraged his son before taking the difficult decision to send him to England to further his snooker education and give him the best chance of fulfilling his potential.

And Ding, a shy kid obsessed with video games and Jackie Chan movies and unable to speak a word of the language, arrived in Northamptonshire and the Rushden Snooker Centre under the watchful eye of Garry Baldrey and Keith Warren, where he practised with among others the 2002 world champion Peter Ebdon.

I was probably one of if not the first journalists to interview Ding at length at 16 for the *Daily Express* with the help of a translator, and he lived, breathed and dreamt snooker, and snooker alone at that time, sharing a house in Wellingborough.

But I left that day with a profound sense of how much more difficult it was for overseas players to make their mark – leaving home at a such a young age, and being pitched into a totally different culture and environment to chase their dream because of the better practice facilities and partners available, and the proximity of the qualifying events. It was hard enough just to play the game.

Being tipped as the "Tiger Woods of snooker", as happened to Ding, probably wasn't always helpful although in fairness he may well not have known about it. But Ebdon, especially, knew exactly how good Ding was. In the *Daily Express* in April 2005 he said: "I practised a lot with Ding as a 15-year-old in the build-up to the defence of my world title in 2003, and he was slaughtering me. We have a superstar on our hands who could win ten World Championships."

In December 2005 in the same newspaper, Ebdon said: "Ding is a big occasion player, he hated playing in Prestatyn in front of no one in qualifiers, the sooner he gets himself in the top 16 the better. Deep down he knows exactly how good he is, and he has a bit of mardiness that all great players have. Ronnie O'Sullivan gets the hump with himself even when he is playing outstanding snooker because he is not happy with his level of performance, and Ding is like that – there is a bit of Ronnie in him. These guys want perfection."

But though Ding was widely tipped as a future world champion, a poor initial record at the Crucible raised doubts as to whether that would ever happen.

Over time, and with a move to Sheffield in 2006 that saw his mother come over to look after and cook for him, Ding showed his ability. He created a sensation by winning a first ranking title at 18 as a wild-card at the China Open, beating Stephen Hendry 9-5 in the final.

Ding never saw a penny of the £30,000 first prize because of his wild-card status, though a canny sponsor in China stepped up to publicly make sure he received a five-figure sum.

And he had followed that up with three more ranking titles including two successes at the UK Championship, before a first Masters title in January of 2011.

Coming in to this World Championship Ding could draw on a good season, reaching the semi-finals of the China Open won by Trump, as well as the Masters title and three further ranking-event quarter-final appearances.

But would that make up for a dismal record in his by-now adopted city of Sheffield, where he had only won two matches in four attempts, and never got past the last 16?

The answer was yes. Ding easily beat Scotland's Jamie Burnett 10-2 in the first round, and then broke new ground by reaching the quarter-finals with a thrilling 13-12 victory over Stuart Bingham, showing the intestinal fortitude some claimed he lacked by winning the last four frames.

Another tough test lay in wait in the form of Mark Selby, but again Ding stepped up and following a 13-10 win was in the semi-finals.

And there he would face Trump, who had continued to surf the wave of self-belief and confidence from Beijing all the way into the last four in Sheffield. Trump took advantage of his 'free shot' against defending champion Robertson by beating him 10-8.

And after that, playing in a cavalier and attacking style that was drawing rave reviews and creating a surge in interest in the tournament, the young prince took out Martin Gould (13-6) and Graeme Dott (13-5). If anything, it had been getting easier for Trump.

But now he was going up against Ding, the player he was looking to topple in more ways than one, not least trying to replace him as the most successful young player in the sport. It was a straight head to head, the fearless attacking approach of Trump, and the break-building and cue ball control of Ding, seen as second only to Ronnie O'Sullivan in that department. It meant that when on song, Ding hardly ever had to play a difficult shot.

Ding already knew he was in better shape for this showdown than when he first appeared at the Crucible in 2007. He says: "I had learned a lot from those first years playing at the World Championship, and didn't feel so bad by 2011.

"On my debut it was very special, it was all new, and I was more nervous. I wasn't used to the format and the long games, plus I felt a lot of pressure from the spectators being so close.

"But by this year I was calmer and not worrying so much about the outcome, able to relax more while I played. Before, I got very frustrated when I was behind, I could get anxious, and was not able to concentrate, but now it seemed different.

"And I felt able to win matches from far behind as well as being a front-runner, so those victories before the semi-final, especially against Stuart Bingham, gave me a lot of confidence."

The left-handed Trump would have fancied himself against anyone at that stage, such was his burgeoning self-confidence and belief. And he viewed the chance to put a marker down with rival Ding as a huge motivator with both looking to get a first world title on the board.

He says: "It was obviously a very tough first-round draw but I was confident once I saw how I was playing and managed to come up with important breaks at the right times throughout the match.

"And from then on I just felt like I was blasting through the draw, it was like being on a wave and I didn't want to get off. I beat Martin Gould pretty easily, and then Graeme Dott, a former world champion, to get into the semi-finals.

"These were good players I was playing but I didn't expect to lose, I don't know if you'd call that confidence, arrogance, or just a growing belief in your own ability. And it was all heading towards a semi-final with Ding after he managed to get past Mark Selby.

"Ding and I were and still are often thought of together because we are close in age, and have some natural ability. And perhaps for that reason I have always thought of it as a bit of a grudge game, he broke through quicker than I did and had that experience of the limelight and the big stages a lot quicker than I did.

"Ding had won the UK Championship and other big ranking tournaments, plus the Masters earlier that year. He was trying to get that World Championship and I had something to prove.

"For me it was a huge occasion in every way, we were both of course very young but already thinking about our careers and that it might be a good idea to get that world title on our CVs early so we could relax a bit."

It was not to be one of those much-hyped sporting encounters that failed to deliver, with Trump still believing to this day that it was one of the best and highest-quality matches he has ever been involved in. When the pair traded century breaks in the first two frames, it set a tone.

Trump suffered his worst session result of the World Championship to that point, losing the second instalment 6-2 to trail 9-7, but even that could not deflect him from his goal.

He recalls: "The standard from the very first frame over the whole 32 frames was very, very high – definitely one of the best matches I have taken part in. And I think it was the new confidence that got me through, my self-belief was so strong and in my head there was no way I was losing it.

"I put everything into it and my potting was brilliant throughout the game.

"Because it was the first time I ever played in the one-table set-up it felt completely different but I felt instantly at home out there, so relaxed. I didn't feel any nerves in that tournament, more than virtually any that I can remember which was strange given the importance.

"No matter what Ding did, and he played very well himself, I resolved to stick with him. I felt good, and every time I got a sight of a ball I was going to go for it, and most of the time I got it.

"Normally there is a bad spell for one player or the other, or both, in a match that long but I really don't think there was in this one. Every frame seemed to be one-visit, or most of them. Both of us were punishing the other.

"Ding played superbly in the second session to end up 9-7 ahead, I didn't play great in the second session – but from that moment onwards in the last two sessions I played really well.

"I had a lot of friends up for that semi-final, and in between sessions we were going out for food and meals together to take my mind off it.

"I am not as relaxed now as I was then about the matches, I do have nerves for the bigger matches. That year I just went for everything and they usually flew in.

"When I look back I am certainly a better all-round player now, but my potting has never been better than it was in that World Championship. If I could replicate that now with my improved safety game I would be coming in with a much better chance in every tournament."

His approach was certainly being lapped up by the crowds in the Crucible, and the millions watching on television. A sensational third session saw Trump make breaks of 123, 102, 71, 61 and 61, while Ding weighed in with runs of 87, 77 and 64. To no one's great surprise, it was 12-12.

While Ding was more than playing his part in a classic contest, he was to tell Chinese journalists afterwards that the whole experience was testing him in new ways – this, after all, the longest match that he had ever played.

He said: "The spectators were all cheering for Judd, I get that a lot and I'm used to it, after all it's on their soil. I won't protest. I've got Chinese students and journalists that come here as supporters even in the UK and that makes me happy enough.

"The long matches, I think I am growing white hair, it's like being tortured playing this, maybe too long. I think maybe best of 19 frames for the first few rounds and then best of 25 for the final would be good enough.

"But in this match Judd showed the abilities he has, especially potting where he is very accurate. He was very clinical and cleared up from any tiny chance. He was also very motivated, perhaps because he hadn't won so much at that time.

"I was very pleased with the standard I produced until right at the end, but the tournament felt enormously long and dragging."

The match had been very close with the pendulum swinging first one way and then the other, but the climax was approaching. Ding put himself in charge by winning three frames in a row with breaks of 138, 47 and 119 to lead 15-14. But that is when Trump showed his mettle, while for the first time the Chinese player showed signs of weakness.

In the next three frames Ding was in first, but managed to lose all of them. And of the three, both players were to agree afterwards that frame 31 was the one that broke Ding's resistance.

The frame before Ding played a loose positional shot on a red on a break of 48, and was forced to play safe off the pink instead of clearing up. He did get other shots, but left the yellow on escaping from a snooker. It was 15-15.

And then with the tension mounting Ding threw in a really bad, nervy miss on a red when leading 27-0 and Trump made 68, a break that was good enough to help him move 16-15 ahead. Trump was now sure he would win.

And he got over the line in the 32nd and final frame. Once again Ding was first in with a great opening red, but a bad contact on a later red triggered a chain of events that saw him the wrong side of the blue, and clipping the brown with the cue ball going in and out of baulk. Losing the safety exchange, Trump cleared up with 105, a fitting final flourish.

Trump clenched his fist and punched the air as the key second-last red went down, with the colours sent fizzing into the pockets in exhibition style to the delight of the crowd.

Ding says: "I just remember the shot I played against Judd on the red at 15-15. The red knocked another red but the position wasn't on the pink.

"I remember that bad shot but it is hard to remember anything else, like how good a match it was. With that shot I could have gone 16-15 because I was on a break – it was a key shot.

"All I remember after that is Judd's potting, he potted everything. When I was young all I wanted to do was go and win world titles like Stephen Hendry. At this time I don't know the special feeling of winning a world title because I haven't lifted the trophy yet. I'll try to do it, it would be a perfect thing."

But if Ding was left desolate, Trump was ecstatic about reaching his first Crucible final, the way he had played, and the nerve he had found when under the most intense pressure at the death in the biggest match of his life to that point.

He says: "It was tit for tat virtually the whole match but I do think the ball he missed at 15-15 was a key one. He was in and missed a bad red and I made a break to go 16-15 up when I probably should have been behind.

"When he missed that it was the first time either of us had looked as if we might be feeling the pressure after all that time and four sessions. It was a really easy one, and it made me think this was a chance, I had to win this frame and that maybe I had him.

"There was so little in it but I just handled the pressure slightly better at the end, and he missed literally a couple of balls that cost him. It is a match that I take a lot of pride from, one of my best wins, and a time when someone played really well against me but I still managed to win.

"It will always be special for me despite what had happened in China, this was the World Championship, the stage I had always wanted to play on and I had got to the final with a high-class performance that had entertained the crowd.

"Ding was and is still one of the players with the most ability out there, he doesn't always show the consistency but on his day he is as good as anyone.

"When you look at what Ronnie O'Sullivan and John Higgins have achieved of those still playing at this time, and Ding is maybe just behind them with the likes of Mark Selby."

Chapter 19

John Higgins v Judd Trump, 2011, final

"The entrance and atmosphere as we came out for the final session, I will remember until my dying day – I have never been close to sampling anything like that at a game of snooker"

THE final of the 2011 World Championship provided one of the classic sporting match-ups, in the form of a young pretender with designs on the throne in Judd Trump, and a three-time world champion and proven course-and-distance winner in Scotland's John Higgins.

And it was not just for that reason that this was one of the most keenly anticipated contests at the Crucible for years – one that delivered on every level. Trump's emergence on the biggest stage, still surfing a wave of confidence and self-belief stemming from his debut ranking-title success in Beijing at the China Open, had been little short of sensational.

A fearless approach, slightly reminiscent of Shaun Murphy's run to the world title in 2005 but if anything taking things up a notch, had delighted and lured in new fans and television viewers, and via Twitter and social media attracted praise from the world of celebrity, including entrepreneur and host of hit TV show *The Apprentice*, Lord Sugar.

Trump's prodigious shot-making had been one of the two major stories of the tournament, and carried him through to and beyond the thrilling semi-final against Ding Junhui featured in Chapter 18 to a first world final.

And there he would meet Higgins, going for a fourth world title and a third in five years, having taken nine years to claim his second in 2007. And the passage of Higgins through to the showpiece provided the other compelling narrative.

To recap Higgins, by this time 35, saw corruption and match-fixing charges dropped at an independent tribunal in September 2010 following a sting operation by the first discredited and now defunct *News of the World*. In the clear on those more serious charges Higgins had, though, spent six months of the season banned after being found guilty of giving the impression he might breach betting rules, and failing to report an illegal approach after his ill-fated trip with former manager Pat Mooney to Kiev in April of 2010.

It was a trip that came after his defeat to Steve Davis at the World Championship, as documented in Chapter 16. Higgins insisted during and after the tribunal that he never had and never would fix a match or a frame for money.

In an additional and very personal blow, Higgins' beloved father and No.1 supporter John Sr, a popular and respected figure around both the junior and professional circuits for more than two decades, was starting to lose his long battle with cancer.

On his return to the tour in November 2010, Higgins could hardly have been in more emotional turmoil, and no one knew just how he would react. They should have known better.

Higgins, quite simply, was a machine – sweating a pint of blood not just for every frame but almost every shot for the rest of the season. The intensity and determination were awesome to behold, and allied to his ability far too good for most. In major tournaments – ranking events, the Masters and the two European Players Tour Championship entries in Hamm and Prague – he had lost just three significant matches out of 33 coming in to the Crucible final.

The first Major back in the fold was the UK Championship in Telford with his father unable to travel, and Higgins incredibly fought back from 9-5 down to beat a rejuvenated Mark Williams 10-9 in a wonderful final.

"Maybe it was fate," said a tearful Higgins in the arena. He added in the *Daily Record*: "I was a man on a mission. I was really determined to try and stop anything which prevented me from winning it. Given everything that surrounded it, this is my finest hour on the table. It means everything, just to be back playing and winning. It means a great deal. Obviously it means a great deal to my family as well." Afterwards a reluctant Higgins sat down with a small group of journalists and opened up over the agonies of the previous six months, earning him considerable respect for doing so.

After pulling out of the German Masters and flying home from Berlin to be with his family as his father passed away, Higgins was persuaded by his mother to do his memory proud by playing in the Welsh Open only days after the funeral. And holding himself together in barely credible fashion Higgins again came through to lift the trophy for another emotional win. You could not have anything but deep admiration for Higgins in Newport, in what must rank as another of the most difficult tournaments of his life. To end up winning it showed real character.

So by the time Higgins arrived at the Crucible he had barely lost a match of consequence since his return, and once in Sheffield overcame Stephen Lee, Rory McLeod, Ronnie O'Sullivan and then Williams in the semi-finals. In the Williams match a spectator had heckled Higgins, referring to the Kiev trip and calling him "a disgrace". Visibly hurt and presumably seething inside, Higgins managed to shrug off an incident that did feel at the time as if it might have been staged.

And he was both up for the challenge of taking on tournament sensation Trump, and wary of his weapons. It was also set to be a final of contrasts, the joyful approach of Trump up against the grimmer determination and supreme matchplay of Higgins. After the semi-final win over Williams, Higgins said in his press conference: "It would be unbelievable to win the World Championship again, incredible. It has been a long year...but I have Judd Trump against me and I don't know where I am going to be able to put the white safe.

"He pots, and pots, and pots. But he is great for the game and Barry Hearn just seems to have the Midas touch. He takes charge and along comes this lad, plucked from the sky and the new wonder-boy our sport badly needs. I am really looking forward to the final.

"You can tell especially from the way that Judd beat Mark Selby in the China Open final recently, and then Neil Robertson in the first round here, that he has it in him to clear up with just one chance. It is a special quality and not many have it. This is going to be as hard as any final I have ever played in."

Trump, for his part, could not wait to get going. He says: "A world snooker final isn't like say a World Cup final in football where you have a few days to prepare and think about it. You finish on the Saturday afternoon or even evening – afternoon against Ding in my case – and then you're on the next day.

"I wasn't tired even at that point, I was buzzing after the semi-final but still felt fairly fresh and was fully focused on finishing the job and winning it. In my head at that time I expected to beat anyone I played, and I was quickly looking ahead to the final.

"Even though I had huge respect for John I was very confident of beating him in that final beforehand. I just felt that if I could carry my form from the whole tournament into the final then I would win it. And that is almost how it turned out, my level just dipped a bit on the second day and John found something as he often does.

"It was an amazing occasion in the final, virtually everyone that I grew up with and that had ever helped me came up, and I felt at home in that atmosphere. It was just a case of getting down to business, and I felt it was my time to break through."

John Higgins v Judd Trump

It became abundantly clear from the start that Trump was not about to ditch the 'all guns blazing' attitude that had got him into the final in the first place. He won the first two frames to settle any nerves, and after Higgins pegged him back made a break of 102 to level at 3-3.

There was irritation for Trump in frame seven, missing a very difficult red to the middle pocket when going for a maximum 147 on a break of 64 and seeing Higgins steal it on the black, but he levelled at 4-4 with a break of 47.

And it was in the second and evening session of the Sunday that Trump cut loose, with some *prima facie* examples of the superb potting that had delighted audiences throughout the tournament.

In frame 10, trailing 5-4, Trump produced a brilliant pot together with deep screw on the third-last red, enabling him to snooker Higgins and then clear up to the pink. In the next there was another superb long pot on frame ball, after an earlier run of 58.

And in frame 12 Trump had the crowd on their feet with a sizzling exhibition, a break of 103 that included a final pink played right-handed and then a black slammed into the green pocket from 11 feet away. That made it 7-5 at the interval, three frames in a row, and John Parrott, sitting in the BBC studio, observed: "This interval is important now for John Higgins to regroup because Judd is starting to jump all over him."

Higgins did just that, but Trump responded once again to take the last three of the night and lead 10-7 overnight.

The standard on the second day, and the third session on the Monday afternoon, went up again. But Higgins was himself starting to motor and Trump was left berating himself for one shot above all other in the match in the 22nd frame, with him still leading 12-9.

Trump had trailed 47-18 but constructed a break of 37 and looked a good bet to steal the frame and hand out what would have been, according to BBC commentator Dennis Taylor, "a real body-blow to John".

The final blue was near the cushion and Trump was not on it well after potting the brown. John Virgo, next to Taylor in the box, intoned: "Surely not even Judd Trump can take this blue on down the cushion, it is too risky and percentage-wise odds-against."

But after huge deliberation and an almost unheard-of two minutes on the shot, Trump took it on with the rest. He probably should have played safe, and not only missed the blue but left it over the pocket for Higgins to close to 12-10. It was the first of what would prove five frames in a row for Higgins, and for Trump the turning point.

Higgins finished the third session with breaks of 93, 113 and 57 to put him 13-12 up going in to the evening climax.

Trump says: "About midway through the third session it started to wobble a bit for me and there was that really bad miss on a blue that cost me a possible 13-9 lead, after which John got on a roll. And if that had gone in and I kept the momentum going, things could have been different.

"On day one and at the start of session three I felt in control of the match. But that blue, as well as costing me that frame the whole course of the match seemed to change in that instant, and little things that had been going for me were not any more. I will always think that one shot changed everything, and from then on John just got stronger and stronger."

The deafening reception given to the two players by the crowd as they walked down the steps that night was something the players themselves, and everyone present, will never forget.

Whether it was the quality of the match, or the shot in the arm Trump had given the sport over the 17 days, it is hard to say with certainty but even the vastly experienced Higgins was left smiling and shaking his head in disbelief in his chair as the applause refused to dampen.

In his post-match press conference, he admitted: "The entrance for us as we came out tonight, I will remember until my dying day. I have never been close to sampling anything like that at a game of snooker. I thought I had been involved in a lot of big matches but that blew it away, by 100 times the best entrance and atmosphere I have ever experienced.

"And in my view a lot of that is down to Judd, he is going to bring an army of fans into the game because of the way he plays. We have got a new star."

Trump, who despite Higgins' loyal body of fans had been the crowd favourite during the match, was similarly moved. He says: "I realise more now looking back on it just what a reception we got, because, and John agreed, I have never heard anything like it before or since. And hopefully the impact I made and the way I had been playing contributed to that. The first three sessions were amazing but the last session was off the scale, at another level. And it was glancing over at John that made me realise, he was looking around and couldn't believe it with all his years playing the game."

Trump never gave up, levelling at 14-14 and pulling back to 16-15 behind, but his own assessment was close to the mark – the tide had turned, and it was running Higgins' way. And the finish, when it came, was applied with characteristic aplomb.

With Higgins leading 17-15 and one away from the title Trump was in first and led 60-0 only to miss an easy pink off the spot. Another red left Higgins needing two snookers but the Scot took the colours up to the pink meaning he needed only one to be able to win. Having skilfully laid it behind the black, the only other ball on the table, Trump missed with his escape and Higgins doubled the pink and potted the black for a famous triumph.

As at the UK Championship and Welsh Open getting over the winning line saw the emotions pouring out of Higgins – finally released, after being channelled for so long on the tournament. But after some tears and being able to share the moment with his wife and children, the smile soon returned as he paraded the trophy.

After 12 months that had tested him in every way, Higgins said after the match: "This is by far and away the biggest and best world title that I have ever won, no question. If my dad had been on my mind too much out there during the match, I wouldn't have been able to play the way I did. But he has been there in the back of my thoughts all the time and he'll be up there having a party. It was motivation to do it for him subconsciously, obviously it was.

"I was always going to go for the double on the pink, last year it was a double from Steve Davis that knocked me out really so to pull one off and win it is unbelievable.

"If someone had said I'd be top of the money list after missing up to 15 tournaments when I was back playing I'd have laughed at them. Just now I am in the moment, but when I sit down and reflect it will all hit me, it's trying to get through everything."

But he was generous in his praise of runner-up Trump, adding: "I think Judd is a future multiple world champion, he is that good. The progress that he has made from winning in China to now is incredible. It was a joy to watch him for me and everyone else, and that can only be good for the game. He's a good looking boy, young and exciting, so it's all set up for him."

Later, Higgins also acknowledged that he might struggle to completely leave behind him the events of the previous year. He said: "I have to accept I will have to contend with that for the rest of my life. It's something I will have to put up with. There are always going to be people who think certain things about me. There's nothing I can do about that, I've just focused on my snooker.

"But my dad made me what I am today. He was an inspiration but this one is also for the rest of my family because they have been right behind me. It has been a tough year. They've all been so strong for me, I couldn't have done it without them. I have found out who my friends are – and my wife Denise has been my rock."

Trump, with a £125,000 runners-up cheque in his pocket, was a cheerier losing finalist than many you see, knowing that the last five weeks, the win in China and his run at the Crucible, had changed his life beyond recognition. He was able to take huge comfort from that.

He said in the post-match press conference: "A few shots here and there changed the match but I went out there and played my game the way I had been, and I am glad I didn't change it for the final.

"I tried my best and it just wasn't good enough. I wasn't tempted to rein it in for the final, I felt I was going to pot every ball I went for. If I had felt differently, maybe I wouldn't have gone for them.

But those shots got me this far and to change my game plan just for the final would have been stupid.

"I enjoyed it, I think the crowd enjoyed it and enjoyed seeing me play over the 17 days, that makes me happy and want to play the game. I was loving it out there. You get nerves when you are scared of missing, but I had won so many matches recently that I wasn't scared of missing. Some of my shots went in, some didn't.

"I want to give the crowd a good show and bring people in. Ronnie O'Sullivan was the person that did that that brought me into snooker, and I'd like to do that.

"In fact the support and attention I got was an insight into what Ronnie has had all his career, it was incredible. It felt like everyone was supporting me even though that wasn't the case, that is how it felt and I have never experienced that again since.

"I'll do something a bit flash with the money, you have to reward yourself – it all depends on car insurance! I have done well in the last two tournaments, so I'll probably have a look at an Audi R8 or a Lamborghini."

It was the year Trump entered the fast lane, but he could not prevent Higgins, unquestionably one of the greatest players of all time emerging from his toughest year, from taking the chequered flag in a final that will be talked about for years to come.

Chapter 20

Neil Robertson v Ronnie O'Sullivan, 2012, quarter-final

"Ronnie had been working with Steve Peters, and I honestly think if this match had taken place 12 months earlier he would have self-destructed under the pressure I was putting him under"

WHEN Ronnie O'Sullivan took on Australian Neil Robertson at the Crucible at the 2012 World Championship, the match represented many separate and clearly identifiable things.

First of all, there was the obvious. It was a huge contest between snooker's most high-profile star in O'Sullivan, and a growing force and arguably the most improved player on tour in Robertson, for a place in the semi-finals. Every time the Rocket, by this time aged 36, reached the latter stages of the blue-riband tournament the event experienced an extra frisson running through its core. He remained the player most fans and television viewers wanted to see, and broadcasters, while publicly of course staying neutral in their studio utterances, were always desperate to see O'Sullivan stay in the draw until at least the quarter-finals in Sheffield.

The three-time world champion was box office, and box office meant ratings, even if he was not always the easiest player to secure late at night or early in the morning to film trailers and previews for the next match.

And on paper in this particular renewal of the biggest tournament on the calendar, with due respect to the others making up the last eight, this had the look of a final in all but name.

However, things had not been going well for O'Sullivan, on or off the table, for a number of years coming in to 2012.

He had not won a ranking title after the 2009 Shanghai Masters until lifting the trophy at the German Masters in Berlin in February of 2012, more of which later.

But that did not begin to tell the full story of the unease, frustration and disaffection felt by O'Sullivan away from the demands of the professional tour.

A prolonged and draining custody battle, over when and how often he could see his children, with ex-partner Jo Langley had taken a heavy toll on O'Sullivan, and was not over yet.

He had been diagnosed with glandular fever, and even a passing glance at his account in *Running: The Autobiography* (Orion, 2013) sees words used to describe his general state and mood in the winter of 2011 such as "miserable", "run down", "not sleeping" and "exhausted".

In 2011, after many years of saying no to the idea mooted by then manager Django Fung, O'Sullivan finally agreed to meet with sports psychiatrist Dr Steve Peters, an athlete turned mental mentor, and renowned for his highly successful work with the British Cycling team – brought in by Sir David Brailsford, and dragging higher performance levels out of so many including Sir Chris Hoy and Victoria Pendleton.

Peters adhered to theories about managing the mind in the arena of sport and had written a book called *The Chimp Paradox*. In this world, the brain was split into a human side and a 'chimp' side, with the chimp controlling emotional reaction and activity, and risking catastrophe if allowed to run amok and unchecked.

The chimp though, so the theory went, was also essential, as without it there was a danger the human side, the one that dealt with reason and logic, could dominate at the expense of spontaneity – risking an approach that verged into the over-cautious, and even the boring.

This language all made perfect sense to O'Sullivan from the outset as he battled with the various and often conflicting demons of keeping himself interested, entertaining the crowd, trying to ensure his emotional side was not too destructive, and actually winning the matches and titles to do his huge talent justice.

But until February 2012 and Berlin, even though the relationship was developing well with Peters hammering home the message that a player could not always be brilliant and there were times to hang in there and mentally switch off, there had been little to show for it in silverware terms.

Then came the now famous first-round match against Andrew Higginson at the Tempodrom, when O'Sullivan trailed 4-0. At many times in his career, there would have been no coming back against a far lower-ranked opponent, and the towel would have been at least metaphorically chucked onto the table. But not this time.

O'Sullivan somehow won that match 5-4, going on to beat Stephen Maguire in the final in a high-class match to claim a first ranking title for two and a half years. Finally there was tangible evidence that Peters might effectively hand O'Sullivan a second career.

But the Crucible, and the 17-day marathon, would once again be the ultimate testing ground. And there was plenty on it for Robertson, too.

Unlike many players who were beaten almost before they started against O'Sullivan, and especially in Sheffield, Robertson was now made of sterner stuff. The Melbourne-born player genuinely believed a second world title was within his grasp this year, and saw the winner of this quarter-final as the overwhelming favourite to lift the trophy that year.

The season 2011–12 had not been Robertson's best in ranking tournaments, one of very few in his 'third crack' at the tour that had not seen him win one of those titles. However, he had won the prestigious Masters invitational event at Alexandra Palace for the first time, marking him out as one of those with a real chance of glory at the World Championship.

Robertson, who had assiduously been picking the brains of any former world champion who would give him the time of day in an effort to improve his game, says: "I was very confident coming in to the World Championship that year. I had a good, very consistent season. I won a couple of the Players Tour Championship tournaments, one in Poland and one in Ireland.

"And of course I had won the Masters for the first time in January, having played well and got a good 10-6 win over Shaun Murphy in the final. That had given me the second leg of the Triple Crown of major BBC events that I wanted badly, and was to go on to achieve in later years.

"And perhaps more importantly I was playing really well and had taken my game to the next level in areas like break-building, safety play and tactical know-how. I felt as if I was becoming the complete all-round player now rather than someone who knocked in long reds and could pot pretty much anything on the table."

O'Sullivan was typically frank about the personal challenges he faced coming in to the 2012 World Championship – delighted at making breakthroughs with Peters, but not fully believing in his heart of hearts that even such progress would be enough to see off Robertson, or win a fourth world title.

He says: "Listen, I had had a lean time of it for a while coming in to that 2011–12 season. I hadn't won a world title since 2008.

"I had a lot of problems and issues off the table, and I had lost some confidence on it, not just in my ability to win the tough matches, but in my ability to deal with situations and the unique pressures and scrutiny I faced in the sport.

"There was a break-up with my ex and a lot of unpleasant stuff going on there, going to court and so on. For two years that really harmed my playing prospects, I couldn't really focus on playing, I just wanted out.

"With things going badly I ended up finally meeting with Steve Peters, something my former manager had been suggesting for a while. And while I was listening and my practice game got better, there hadn't really been clear benefits showing in my results.

"I played well in the minor PTC events and won a couple of those, but not so well in the major events. Then it came to the UK Championship and I played Steve Davis in the first round and just thought to myself, 'I played well, there.'

"Then I played Judd Trump in the second round and although I played solid match snooker I lost 6-5 and came away feeling maybe like Stephen Hendry did a few times, thinking, 'Maybe I haven't got it any more.' I felt like I played a good game but I had lost.

"I wasn't used to that, although obviously it had happened a few times in my career, usually if I played well, I won. I was really starting to think I hadn't got it in the tank any more to beat the best players in big matches.

"And that was something that Steve Peters and I worked a lot on in those first months, not to listen to those voices, that it was a roll of the dice, you win some and you lose some in sport but don't read more into it than that and trust your talent and keep working hard in practice.

"I remember saying to him again and again, 'I am not used to playing well and losing,' so we had to get a grip on that mindset. We stuck at it, but I was being tested, especially after Trump beat me again 6-2 at the Masters.

"Was this a new era for snooker that I just wasn't cut out to deal with and keep up with these guys?

"But I got my break in Germany, from being 4-0 down against Andrew Higginson in the first round. I was also something like 63-0 down at 4-1, and cleared up with a 67, went on to win 5-4, and then ended up winning a first ranking title for three years or so beating Maguire in the final.

"I had won the Premier League but that was a shot-clock and different, I had won it so many times it was almost my event. It was virtually a banker at the start of the season.

"It was a career-changing moment, because mine had been going nowhere. I was never going to win another title the way I was thinking about things, and it was proof to me that what Steve was telling me was working.

"I followed it up by playing well at the Welsh Open, losing to Mark Selby in the semis, but I played well and beat good players. And even in China I was cueing well, Maguire beat me 5-4 but I was feeling good again.

"However in my heart of hearts, even feeling much better mentally and playing better, I still didn't truly believe that at the Crucible, at the World Championship and over 17 days, I could hold it together and win a fourth world title."

Once the match was into the second session, by which time O'Sullivan had started to motor, Robertson was already sensing that the by now not-so-secret weapon, Peters, had made a huge and positive impact on O'Sullivan's mindset and outlook.

He continues: "It was always going to be a decent-quality match, with both of us confident and playing well. And that was the case in the first session of the match. I was 5-3 in front, had made a century and some other breaks, and was feeling good. But Ronnie was also looking in good form, he too had made a century break and had a 93 to go 3-3. But those last two frames of the session were important and gave me a lot more belief.

"Ronnie had been working with Dr Steve Peters for a few months, and I honestly think if this match had taken place 12 months earlier he would have self-destructed under the pressure I was putting him under. But as we had seen from his amazing charge to the title in Berlin after being all but out of the German Masters in the first round, this was a different animal now.

"I think he would have got frustrated in that two- or three-year lull he had, because I was playing good safety, varying the tempo of the match and counter-attacking well, clearing up after he had made a mistake, the kind of breaks and frames that can get to you and can hurt.

"But maybe it was crucial that he had seen Steve Peters' methods working and bearing fruit the way they had in Germany earlier that year.

"In the second session you really saw just what a good place he was in. Under real pressure he came out and played very aggressively, and really put me on the back foot. He wasn't playing recklessly, but just challenging me with almost every shot.

"Of course he had the crowd right behind him, because he hadn't won the world title for four years and hadn't looked like winning it again to be honest for some of that time. That's the thing playing Ronnie at the Crucible, you are not just playing him, you are playing the crowd as well and it is something you cannot know until you have experienced it.

"In my career he is quite simply the only player in the world where you experience that. I get my fair share of support, 50-50 at worst usually, and even when I am not their favourite I am quite good at shutting it out and focusing, but apart from maybe Ding in China to a lesser extent there is nothing like it out there.

"There is just an extra buzz about the match and the tournament, especially in Sheffield, when he is involved. I would compare it to tennis. Andy Murray did brilliantly in tennis in 2016 but no one makes a tournament come alive like Roger Federer. No one. He gets incredible support and it comes from the way he goes about it, the shot-making, he is a bit of an enigma, and says what he thinks.

"Ronnie won the six frames in a row, hardly missing anything and leaving me in all sorts of trouble when I came to the table, so that was 9-5 down from 5-3 up. And in the end I was delighted to get the final two frames of the afternoon session and not fold, to make it 9-7 ahead of the evening."

O'Sullivan had developed a new-found respect for this new and improved version of Robertson, the one that could now mix it up, slow things down, and still clear the table as well as anyone. And after the first session all his homework with Peters was called upon, as belief he could win the match let alone the title was tested to its limits.

But those significant hurdles were overcome, and a sublime second session meant that the match was O'Sullivan's to lose, something he never looked like allowing to happen.

O'Sullivan says: "This 2012 World Championship was the first supreme test of all the work I had been doing with Steve. There is no bigger battleground than the Crucible for us, it is the biggest stage in Sheffield, and where you feel the heat of the battle like nowhere else.

"I had done okay during the season, but this was different.

"And I remember against Robertson being 5-3 down after the first session, and thinking very clearly, 'I am not playing well enough to beat this guy.' I thought he was strong and had the measure of me, I was lucky to be only 5-3 down.

"I expected more of it in the next two sessions, but I had got to the quarters and that was okay. I was already getting my excuses ready in my head, it hadn't been a bad season, I had made progress and steps forward on the table and mentally, I could live with all that. That is what I was thinking.

"I honestly did not believe that I could win another world title, not before the event, not before that match, and certainly not after that first session. I had told Steve I would LIKE to win another one, that it would be my dream to win another two, but I didn't expect it.

"But he told me, 'If you want another two, that's the goal,' and I ended up winning two in the first two years I worked with him, rather than the two in six we had talked about.

"As well as that target I set myself another of winning a world title in my 40s – I was only 36 at the time. But in this match any early optimism had gone once it got to 5-3 to Neil. I just didn't think I could compete with him, he had grown into a really strong opponent.

"But in the second session I found something, some rhythm, some form, and I upped my pace and my tempo and won six straight frames to go 9-5 up, before he got it back to 9-7. And suddenly you are thinking 'Aye, aye, I'm in with a chance here.'

"I was sure it would be a 13-12 either way, but I ended up playing even better in the evening and final session, played shots and made breaks that I was proud of under the most pressure. I started to feel it was mine to lose, which I hadn't been feeling.

"And that meant going out there, being a front-runner, and taking the game away from your opponent. I love powering over the line, like Usain Bolt, and I had had two or three years where I hadn't been doing that, more stumbling and twitching over the line.

"That doesn't win you world titles though, so I came out very positive, determined to use the techniques I had been working on with Steve, stay calm – and I played my best session of the whole tournament in that final session. That to me was absolutely massive. It did feel a bit like the final, and I had played really, really well against a very tough opponent who expected to beat me."

O'Sullivan had indeed rediscovered that ability to power over the line under the most intense pressure on the biggest stage, making breaks of 104, 71, 100 and 59 to seal a 13-10 win.

Robertson had done well to get it back to 12-10 from 12-8 down and, still believing he could win, was left to rue a 23rd frame in which a tough missed red to the middle pocket was to cost him dear.

He says: "In the final session I actually played okay, but he punished any half-mistake that I made and was finishing the frames in one visit. He made a couple of centuries and a 71 to go 12-8 up and obviously at that time the game looks up and you are really staring down the barrel.

"I made two very good breaks to get it back to 12-10, so I was never going to give up and if I was going to lose it was to be going down fighting.

"I had a chance of a red in the middle at 12-10. It was tough, but I was sure I would win the frame coming off breaks of 89 and 77, I was in one-visit mode myself, and at 12-11 it really would have been game back on – maybe a 50-50 match. But I missed it, left it, and that was it, he cleared up.

"I honestly believe that I would have beaten anyone else that year. You never know totally, different opponents play different shots, but I was convinced I was going to be world champion that year and win a second world title. And it took Ronnie playing at or near his best to stop me.

"The chances to win world titles don't come along every year, there were years after where I was playing well and making loads of centuries but something else didn't go quite right, so that was a chance.

"To be honest Ronnie was virtually unstoppable that year. I hate losing, everyone knows that about me, and when you are like that and you do lose you try and find reasons, sometimes they may sound like excuses, for why it has happened.

"That year I really fancied it even against Ronnie, and to push him 13-10 when he was playing that well I could live with myself. I did feel it was the real final in some ways, I know some others viewed it that way, and I am sure if I had beaten him I would have gone on to win a second world title that year."

From O'Sullivan's perspective, the feeling that this might have been the 'real' final proved accurate at least in the sense that neither Matthew Stevens nor Ali Carter were able to push him as hard as Robertson. And after Berlin, the methods of Peters had now come through another vital test.

He adds: "After beating Neil I felt very strong, I was into the semis, I was flying in practice and hitting the ball well, and all areas of my game were in good shape. I knew it would now take someone playing very well to beat me.

"And I had seen it in this match and this year of 2012, everything that Steve had said to me about how sport goes and how you have to keep on an even keep whatever crops up. Going in to a match with no confidence, losing a first session, believing I wasn't good enough, but being strong mentally to come back and play well and win – turning it around in 24 hours.

"And that was a big thing for me, keeping that thought that things could turn around, before I didn't have that in the locker if I wasn't playing well and that can lead to you almost giving up. I didn't take the thoughts from the first session into the second session.

"And I realised, and I know this is going to sound a bit strange, but maybe for the first time truly that talent is not enough. To win titles you must have the right mindset and it helped give me almost a second career from 2012.

"The likes of Hendry, John Higgins, Steve Davis were born with it. I wasn't born with it, and had to work on it and discover it for myself.

"And fate dictated that I met someone who was able to get into my head and get a lot more out of me in terms of wins, titles and doing myself justice.

"To beat Neil and then go on and win the title that year was better than winning the first one, much sweeter. I had to really work for it, and come through some periods of real self-doubt. I came off after the final and was fresh as a daisy, and was ready to go again. It had felt easy, how I had played and managed myself emotionally.

"I think of it like an F1 driver managing what is left in the fuel tank, or on the tyres. For me it is emotions. It wasn't going all out and dying on the table, but pacing myself through a season, and a tournament. The dips and troughs were less severe.

"And I had learned that sometimes not winning wasn't a catastrophe, that turning up and playing to the best of your ability was okay and worthwhile. Sometimes it is not your turn.

"So it wasn't just the winning, it was how I had dealt with everything. And having my little boy there after the final made it even more amazing, I so wanted him and my daughter there to be there and see me win, and I had begun to think it wouldn't happen.

"I was welling up during the last frame and it felt like just me and my son in there at one point. It felt like something that wasn't meant to happen."

Bibliography and research

Personal interviews (2016–17)
Thanks go to: Cliff Thorburn, Tony Knowles, Steve Davis, Jimmy White, Terry Griffiths, Dennis Taylor, Joe Johnson, Stephen Hendry, Ronnie O'Sullivan, Peter Ebdon, Brandon Parker, Ken Doherty, Shaun Murphy, Matthew Stevens, Neil Robertson, Martin Gould, Ding Junhui, Judd Trump, Mike Watterson and Barry Hearn.

Books:
Alex Higgins, *My Story: From the Eye of the Hurricane*, Headline, 2007
Steve Davis, *Interesting: My Autobiography*, Ebury Press, 2015
Jimmy White – *Second Wind: My Autobiography*, Trinity Sports Media, 2014
Ronnie O'Sullivan – *Running: The Autobiography*, Orion, 2013
Crucible Almanac (various years), edited by Chris Downer

Television:
BBC Television footage including *Crucible Classics* series
Life Stories: Jimmy White – ITV (2013)
Life Stories: Ronnie O'Sullivan – ITV (2012)
Alex Higgins: The People's Champion – BBC (2010)

Web sites:
www.cuetracker.net
www.ProSnookerBlog.com
www.snooker.org
www.worldsnooker.com
www.wpbsa.com
www.bbc.co.uk/sport
Youtube footage
Newspapers (referenced at the time)
Daily Express
Daily Record
The Observer

Select Index

Index